Divine Decrees III

Prayer Declarations for Present Day Issues

CLEM ESOMOWEI

authorHOUSE®

AuthorHouse™ UK
1663 Liberty Drive
Bloomington, IN 47403 USA
www.authorhouse.co.uk
Phone: 0800.197.4150

LONDON ENGLAND, U.K.
pastorclem@triumphant.org.uk

Published by AuthorHouse   02/10/2015

ISBN: 978-1-5049-3582-1 (sc)
ISBN: 978-1-5049-3581-4 (hc)
ISBN: 978-1-5049-3583-8 (e)

Library of Congress Control Number: 2015900663

Print information available on the last page.

This book is printed on acid-free paper.

Scripture quotations are from the Holy Bible, King James Version (Authorized Version). First published in 1611. Quoted from the KJV Classic Reference Bible, Copyright © 1983 by The Zondervan Corporation.

Contents

Dedication

Divine Decrees III edition is dedicated to God Almighty, the Esomowei and Amachree families, my darling wife Pastor Marjorie Esomowei and all known and unknown intercessors out there. I give praise to the Great One who ever lives to make intercession for you and me; Jesus Christ the High Priest of our profession. Your prayers, love and care brought me through. Thank You!

Introduction

This third edition adds more pages to the second edition with new topics like 'Prayers Against The Spirit of The Avenger, Prayers Against Terminal Diseases, Prayers For Divine Elevation, Prayers Against Epidemics' and so on. Prayer is the art and act of communicating with God. It is our link with heaven and the realms of the spirit. It is the power source of any human being who desires to succeed God's way. Prayer is our most important Christian duty after righteousness. It is an art because we have to engage in it according to biblical principles. It is an act because prayer cannot be totally delegated but be embarked upon daily and incessantly for individual victory. Communication with our bridegroom becomes a necessity for meaningful relationship. Prayer is the life giving breath of a modern day Christian. God does not do anything without speaking forth and this is the ministry of the prophet. John reveals that, *'in the beginning was the word, and the word was with God, and the word was God* (John1:1-3). God created the universe by spoken word. In the Hebrew language a word represents the very thing spoken because God created all things by His word. The word therefore defines the reality of the object. In the Hebrew the word for object *devarim or dawbar* is the same used for '*word*' because a word does not just represent size, colour, shape but the very spiritual essence since it was the word that brought it into existence. God made Adam to name all the animals He created because Adam had the ability to speak like God and become co-creative by the spoken word. Speaking should be backed up with faith and that's the reason why the spoken word is referred to as the spirit of faith. Our words are not supposed to be empty or void of power. God says, *'so shall my words be that goes forth out of my mouth: it shall not return unto me void, but it shall accomplish that which I please, and it shall prosper in the thing whereto I send it.'* (Isaiah 55:11). The word therefore depicts purpose originally intended by the Creator. Jesus is the word personified and represents the sigma or summation of the purpose of God on earth. That is the reason why every name in heaven and earth must be subject to the name of Jesus Christ and every knee must bow to the name of Jesus Christ. The name of Jesus therefore gives us access to the realms of divine purpose as we pray. We now understand the statement by Jesus Christ, *'the words that I speak unto you, they are spirit and they are life.* (John 6:63b)'

God made His purposes and intentions known through the prophets who spoke forth before the manifestation. God spoke about the seed of the woman bruising the head of Satan, He spoke about a Star coming out of Jacob and a Sceptre rising from Israel being prophetic of Jesus Christ the Messiah. He spoke through prophets Isaiah, Ezekiel, Jeremiah, Micah and many other prophets about the coming of Jesus Christ thousands of years before He actually came. Prophetic words become the mould into which history fits and validates the fact that words create and words represent the raw material for reality. This makes the spoken word very important in the life of a human being. Scripture declares that *'a man's belly shall be satisfied with the fruit of his mouth; and with the increase of his lips shall he be filled: Death and life are in the power of the tongue and they that love it shall eat the fruit thereof* (Proverbs 18:20-21). There is power in the spoken word especially when it lines up with scripture which validates original purpose and intention of God. According to the epistle of Paul to the Hebrews, *'For the word of God is quick, and powerful, and sharper than any twoedged sword, piercing even to the dividing asunder of soul and spirit, and of the joints and marrow, and is a discerner of the thoughts and intents of the heart* (Hebrews 4:12). God confused the contrary vision of those who intended to settle and build a tower to heaven with diverse languages or words and He also used the heavenly language of tongues and diverse tongues to unite the purpose of all those people from different nations in the day of Pentecost. This was after the disciples tarried in continuous release of words in prayers for fifty days. Prayers move the power that moves the world and the effectual fervent prayer of a righteous man avails. A spirit filled believer is so filled with potential power that words released from his or her mouth become activating keys for angels and the Holy Spirit to go on assignment. The angels that excel in strength are waiting for you to open up your mouth and decree, declare, pronounce, prophesy and speak. John the Baptist is described as a voice crying in the wilderness. Jesus Christ declared His purpose as one anointed to preach the gospel to the poor and God is also described as *'He that speaketh from heaven.'* Your mouth is not just meant for delicacies but mainly for divine declarations resulting in total emancipation and progress in every area of life. Just as your mouth is used for taking in physical nutrition, it is also very important for spiritual nutrition, strength and progress. Many live their lives confessing what the devil is doing or what others are saying. Negative words would only create snares in our path. The tongue is described by James as little but controlling the tripartite human being. The perfect person is someone who has control over his or her tongue. God could not use Jeremiah or Isaiah until He touched their tongues. Your present state and stage in life could be directly linked to your speech patterns. Jesus said about the importance of words, *'For by thy words thou shalt be justified, and by thy words thou shalt be condemned* (Matthew 12:37). The Psalmist declares, *'Let the redeemed of the Lord say so whom He has redeemed from the hands of the enemy'* because it is with our mouth we make confession unto salvation and with our hearts we believe unto righteousness. Joshua was told to meditate the word day and night in order to bring down walls and have good success. Meditation has to do with speaking the word of God to yourself. Listed below are several scriptural prayer decrees and declarations covering a wide range of issues that can assist in fulfilling your covenant dreams and make you live triumphantly as a child of God. Since your tongue is the pen of a ready writer, you can write your destiny using your mouth as an instrument to declare God's words concerning you, your Church, your city and your nation. The best way to use these confessions is to take the ones that pertain to your issue(s) and proclaim them when you wake up in the morning and before you go to bed at night. Consistency in doing this will yield fast results. God bless you as you decree.

'We having the same spirit of faith, according as it is written, I believed, and therefore have I spoken; we also believe, and therefore speak'(II Cor. 4:13).

Enter His Courts with Praise

- Father I thank you, I praise you, I give you glory for waking me up today into your glorious destiny for my life.
- I enter into your courts with praise and your gates with thanksgiving.
- I thank you for my life, (my wife/husband), my children, relatives, and friends, colleagues in ministry and church members.
- I thank you in advance for victory over every challenge and issue that would confront me today in Jesus name.
- I love and worship you King of kings, Lord of lords, Alpha and Omega, First and Last, Beginning and the End, The Yes and Amen, The Bigger than the biggest, The Higher than the highest, the unquestionable, wisest, immortal, invisible, but visible God! Ancient of days, The Wheel in the middle of the wheel, My fortress and Firm Foundation, The Unchangeable Changer, I bow before Thee, prostrate, venerate, exalt and extol you, The I Am that I Am, The Rock of ages, Lily of the valleys, Rose of Sharon, Balm in Gilead, Jehovah Rapha, My Healer, Jehovah Elohim, Jehovah Mekadesh, Jehovah Roe, Jehovah El Gibbor, Jehovah Olam, Jehovah Kanna, Jehovah El Elyon, my Shield, my Buckler, my Bulwark, my Strong Tower, True and Faithful, Bread for the hungry, Water for the thirsty, Husband to the widow, Father to the fatherless, the One Who dwells and shines forth between the cherubs. How great Thou art! Justice and judgement are the habitation of thy throne. You are the Holy One of Israel, the Monarch of the universe, the One Who has ordered this praise on my lips, Well done! A thousand tongues are not enough to praise you. We praise, worship and thank you Majesty. Be thou exalted and glorified, Let your glory be upon the earth, Amen!

Victory over Daily Satanic Harassment

- I declare and decree that accidents, drunk drivers, drugged drivers or persons under the influence of devils, witchcraft, occultism, alcohol, terrorists, gangs, unwarranted police confrontation, litigations, libels, court cases, CCJs, bailiffs, speed cameras, traffic infringements, parking tickets, mistaken identity, stray bullets or weapons, robbers, thieves, burglars, devouring spirits, repossession threats, red bills, unnecessary bills and fines is not my portion in Jesus name.
- I trample upon every satanic intimidation against my life in Jesus name.
- I command my spirit soul and body to be strong against of spirit of heart failure, depression and surrender in Jesus name.
- I refuse to quit or give in to every satanic harassment in Jesus name.
- I come against every satanic strategy to frustrate my day using my boss, co-workers, family members, friends, church members, public, government authorities, financial institutions and banks.
- I bind every evil spirit of entanglement and confinement in Jesus name.
- I call forth territorial enlargement in every area of my life today in Jesus name.
- I am going forward in my life today and I bind every spirit of retrogression in Jesus name.
- I pursue, overtake and recover everything concerning my life today in Jesus name.
- Let your kingdom come in my life.
- Let your will be done today and let your kingdom come in every aspect of my life, family, job, business and ministry today.
- I have the life of God flowing through my spirit, soul, body and endeavours.
- I dwell in eternity, therefore eternal life flows through every part of my body.
- My body is quickened by the same Spirit of God that raised Jesus from the dead.

- I nullify and cast out every satanic defilement in my sleep in Jesus name.
- My body, soul and spirit are the temple of the Holy Spirit of the Almighty God Jehovah and His only begotten Son Jesus Christ.
- The joy of the Lord is my strength today in Jesus name
- Today I challenge every challenge, attack every attack, bulldoze every mountain, throw down or leap over every wall, run through every troop, part every Red sea, quench every satanic fire, bend every bow of steel with my hands and return home without injury or deformity in Jesus name.
- I am more than a conqueror in every endeavour of my life in Jesus name.
- I am not a loser but a winner in Jesus name.
- Let the power of God destroy every injection, and objects assigned by Satan and his agents to defile my body, soul and spirit.
- I uproot, throw down and cast out every satanic implantation against my life today in Jesus name
- I bind and cast out every defiling spirit, negative programmes, infirmities, thoughts and imaginations assigned against my spirit, soul and body in Jesus name.
- I cleanse my spirit soul and body with the purifying fire of the Holy Spirit and the blood of Jesus.
- This is the day that the Lord has made and I shall rejoice and be glad in it.
- Father I thank you for giving to me my daily bread in Jesus name.
- I shall not fall into temptation today in Jesus name.
- I plead the blood of Jesus over my day and ask for forgiveness in advance for every sin of my mind and omission in Jesus name.
- I sanctify my spirit, soul, body, thoughts, imaginations, sightings, feelings with the blood of Jesus.
- I serve as unto the Lord with gladness in everything I do today.
- I declare that I am coming back home with testimonies, sound mind, wholeness, praise, victories and spoils of war in my hands because He causes me to triumphant always in Jesus name.

Victory over Prayerlessness

- I bind every satanic spirit, demons and witches assigned to attack and nullify my prayer life in Jesus name.
- I refuse to partake in any meal that will hinder my prayer life in Jesus name.
- I come against spiritual coldness, luke-warmness and prayerlessness in Jesus name.
- I ask God to fill me with the spirit of intercession and spiritual warfare.
- I come against the spirit of heaviness, slumber, spiritual coldness and apathy in Jesus name.
- I open the spiritual magazine of my mouth and soul wide for the Lord to fill with divine words, unction and anointing in Jesus name.
- I declare that my tongue is the tongue of a ready writer because grace is poured on my lips in Jesus name.
- I refuse to quit in prayers before my answer comes in Jesus name.
- I persevere in prayers like Daniel until the Lord brings the answer in Jesus name.
- I must push in prayers without ceasing until something happens and I receive my testimonies in Jesus name.
- I bind every evil spirit assigned against my Bible studies in Jesus name. I shall make time to study the Bible and I pray for spiritual understanding as I read the word.
- Lord, I ask for unction to pray in the Spirit to by-pass every satanic spy and satanic prayer hijackers in my areas of influence, atmosphere, stratosphere and heavenlies.
- I refuse to be entangled by the snare of bitterness, unforgiveness, envy, jealousy, strife, anger, fear and doubt that would hinder my prayers in Jesus name.
- I release everyone who has offended me in Jesus name including …….etc
- I come against every spirit of slumber and distractions assigned against my prayer life and Bible studies in Jesus name.
- I declare that none of my prayers shall fall to the ground nor return void in Jesus name but prosper where it was sent.

- I declare that the words that come out of my mouth in prayer are like, bullets, fireballs, hailstones, intercontinental and interstellar ballistic missiles causing destruction of satanic schemes, wiles, structures and re-creating, re-directing and restructuring what God desires in my life in Jesus name.
- I am spiritually on fire and ready for spiritual warfare at the promptings of my Chief Commander Jesus Christ and the Holy Spirit Who is my Counsellor.

Put on the Whole Armour
of God

- I declare that I am strong in the Lord and the power of His might.
- I put on the whole armour of God against every wile of Satan and his cohorts
- I am triumphant over every satanic wiles.
- I walk in truth as a spiritual belt of integrity and wholeness for my life.
- My mind is renewed in every area of my life.
- I take the Sword of the Spirit which is the word of God as an offensive weapon against every satanic projections, arrows, fiery darts, thoughts and imaginations in Jesus name.
- I refuse to walk in condemnation because I am right standing with God through Jesus Christ who died for my sins.
- I walk in covenant relationship with the great Almighty God Jehovah, Jesus Christ his Son and the Holy Spirit.
- Therefore I cannot fail or be defeated.
- My faith in God quenches every fiery dart, suggestions of evil spirits and evil men trying to pull me back from a life of victory in Jesus Christ.
- I cast down every negative thought, carnal attractions and demonic manipulations of mind control.
- I put on my helmet of salvation to overcome every arguments concerning the promises of God in my life in Jesus name.
- I cast out satanic fowls of the air assigned to neutralise the rhema word of God in my heart in Jesus name.
- I shall grow from one glory of divine revelation to higher realms of revelation.
- The word of God is my Sword of the Spirit against every incursion and transgression of Satan against my life, family and ministry.
- I put on my garment of praise against every spirit of heaviness and mourning in Jesus name.
- I am alert and sensitive in the spirit by the Holy Spirit that dwells in me.
- Lord I thank you for unction to pray with all manner of prayers and supplication in the Spirit for the saints, my acquaintances and family in Jesus name.

- I shall not be overtaken by any satanic attack in Jesus name.
- I am not dull of hearing or seeing because my spiritual ears and eyes shall always be opened to detect any plan of Satan and the wicked against my life, family and ministry.

Confess Manifestation of
Every Gift and Talent

- I walk in the sevenfold manifestations of the Holy Spirit in my life for wisdom, knowledge, understanding, might, counsel reverence, and lordship in Jesus name.
- I desire to walk in the nine gifts of the Spirit of God for the benefit of the church and others who come my way.
- Therefore I thank God for the word of knowledge, word of wisdom, discerning of spirits, working of miracles, gifts of healing, gift of faith, gift of tongues, interpretation of tongues and prophesy in Jesus name.
- Every talent and gift of God in my life shall be manifested in Jesus name.
- Father help me perfect the nine fruit of your Spirit in my life in Jesus name.
- I am filled with the spirit of wisdom and revelation in the knowledge of Him.
- The eyes of my understanding are enlightened and I know the hope of His call and the riches of the inheritance of the saints in the light.
- I am cognisance of the working of the mighty power that God has made available to me which is the same as the power that raised Jesus Christ from the dead.
- I walk in the liberty of Christ and refuse to be bound by human legalism and misinterpretations of the scriptures.
- Father I thank you for helping me stir every gift and talent you have bestowed upon me.
- My gifts and talents shall make room for me in Jesus name.
- I declare that every potential in me shall be used to bless my generation in Jesus name.
- Lord I thank you for helping me put my body under and stay humble as you manifest the talents and gifts in my life in Jesus name.
- The Lord shall use my gifts and talents to meet my financial and material needs in Jesus name.
- I shall not die but live to declare the works and finish the works of God bestowed upon my life in Jesus name.
- I shall not be a cast away at the last day but receive commendation from the Lord, 'Well done thou good and faithful servant.

Declarations for Witnessing

- I am a messenger of the good news of Jesus Christ to everyone who needs salvation.
- I bind every spirit of fear and intimidation trying to stop me from witnessing to others in Jesus name.
- I am blessed anywhere I go because I bring the good news and peace of the gospel to everyone I come in contact with in Jesus name.
- I shall prosper anywhere I go and in everything I do because I am a propagator of the gospel and my feet shall always be beautiful on every mountainous situation.
- God has not given to me the spirit of fear but the spirit of power, love and a sound mind.
- My life, my character, my actions and my words shall be a good witness of Jesus Christ.
- I shall win souls and receive the blessings of wisdom from God.
- My life is a tree of righteousness bearing fruits of salvation.
- I shall not prevent the Holy Spirit from using my lips to witness and win souls into the kingdom of heaven.
- I thank God for the manifestation of the gifts of the Spirit in my life as I witness.
- I believe God to open great and effectual doors of utterance for me in this nation, foreign nations and every continent of the earth in Jesus name.
- I decree that I shall fulfil my part of the divine commission in Jesus name.
- I believe God to directly and indirectly contribute to the propagation of the gospel on earth and win souls through television, radio, crusades, conferences, street evangelisms, mission trips to tune of millions of souls in Jesus name.

Proclaim your Victory over Sickness and Disease

- I am healed supernaturally and miraculously by the stripes of Jesus Christ on the cross of Calvary where he took away all my infirmities, sicknesses and diseases over 2000yrs ago.
- Every disease bearing bacteria, virus or micro-organism that touches my DNA, body fluids, organs, muscles, bones, bone marrow, tissues, nerves, blood vessels, blood or hormones dies instantaneously.
- No previous affliction or calamity shall rise against me the second time in the name of Jesus.
- I shall not die but live to declare the works of God and finish my God given destiny.
- All my organs and body parts including my muscles, bones, bone marrow, hormones, tissues, cells, DNA, lymphatic system, blood cells, pancreas, kidneys, liver, urinary tract, reproductive organs, alimentary canal, thyroid and adrenal glands are functioning fine in the name of Jesus.
- I speak health and vitality by the stripes of Jesus to my medulla oblongata, my cerebral cortex, cerebrum and my cerebellum.
- Every neurone and neurotransmitter in my brain and body nerves is functioning with divine precision in Jesus name.
- I speak divine health to my heart and lungs. I command dangerous cholesterol in my blood to be dissipated and flushed out of my body in Jesus name.
- I command every atherosclerotic blockade in my arteries to melt and disappear from my blood system in Jesus name.
- I claim the blood over everything injected into my body as I eat, drink or receive medical treatment in Jesus name.
- I cancel every effect of food eaten in the dream and declare them null and void. The word says, 'if I eat any deadly thing it shall not harm me' in Jesus name
- I will not eat from the table of spiritual and physical idols in Jesus name. I refuse to defile myself with any satanic meat.
- My alimentary canal, urinary tract, kidneys, reproductive organs shall continue to function according to divine order in my body in the name of Jesus.

- I shall be strong in old age and reject any form of muscle, joint stiffness or arthritis and senile diseases in Jesus name
- Every gallstone in my bladders/kidneys must dissolve supernaturally in Jesus name.
- I reject terminal diseases assigned against my life in Jesus name.
- I have been delivered from pestilences and terminal diseases by Jesus Christ and therefore, I declare that cancer and incurable diseases of any form is not my portion in Jesus name.
- I bind every blood transmitted diseases, HIV and viruses and prevent them from coming in contact with me in Jesus name.
- Every disease bearing germ or virus that touches my body dies instantaneously in the name of Jesus.
- The Spirit of God in me boosts my immune systems against any microbial and viral foreign aggressor in Jesus name.
- When Satan and his agents come against me like a flood, the Spirit of God in me and outside me shall automatically lift up a standard against Satan, his principalities, demons, witches and human agents.
- I am death proofed by the Spirit of God, the word of my testimony and the blood of Jesus Christ.
- I command every death angel to be blinded from my presence and sphere of influence in Jesus name.
- I command every spirit of calamity assigned against my family and I to pass over and miss its target in Jesus name.
- I bind and paralyse every blood sucking spirit and command their teeth to be broken.
- I shall not waste in the bed of languishing but be delivered from every bed of sickness and hospital admissions in Jesus name.
- I return every satanic assignment to sender.
- Let God release his angels to persecute every satanic assignment against my life.
- Let their way be dark and slippery and let the angels of God bind Satan and his agents with chains and fetters of iron in Jesus name. Let them be paralyzed and rendered ineffective in Jesus name.
- Every spiritual, psychological and physical stone, instrument, arrow, dart, weapons formed against me, my family and church members shall not prosper in Jesus name.

- I render them ineffective and I return every one of them back to the senders.
- I exercise my God given dominion and authority over every power of darkness.
- I trample upon every evil spirit and cast them out of my presence in Jesus name.
- I am more than a conqueror because God is for me and no satanic power can conquer me in Jesus name.

Release from Unlawful Captivity

- I declare that Satan the prince of this world has nothing in me.
- I scatter every spiritual and physical padlocks, fetters, chains, crystal balls, basins, pins, knives, weapons, images, caricatures, idols used against me in the satanic world in the name of Jesus Christ.
- I command fire upon every satanic beast and satanic paraphernalia, witches covens, dens, groves, altars, marine dwellings and shrines where my name has been called, is being called or shall be called in Jesus name.
- I scatter every arrest warrant issued against my life in the spirit realm in Jesus name
- I nullify and blindfold every spiritual surveillance over my life, family, job and business in Jesus name.
- I release myself from every lawful captivity of satanic principalities and powers in Jesus name.
- I bind, destroy, denounce, renounce and nullify every covenant, soul tie made knowingly and unknowingly with Satan, principalities, powers, rulers of darkness, spiritual wickedness in high places, familiar spirits, witches and wizards in Jesus name.
- I scatter every satanic stronghold and resistance against my personal, family, social, national, international and global freedom and emancipation in Jesus name.
- I scatter every snare and refuse to be a prey of the terrible in the name of Jesus Christ.
- Every cycle of generational curses is broken in my life and family in Jesus name.
- I declare that Jesus has redeemed me from every lawful captivity and curse of the law when he hung on the cross, died for me and resurrected.
- Because I am more than a conqueror, no weapon formed against me shall prosper or get to its target in Jesus name.
- Every scheme and wile of the enemy and satanic hosts to destabilize my progress is bound, cancelled, cast out and burnt with fire in Jesus name.
- I am free because the truth of the word of Jesus Christ, the blood and the anointing has set me free indeed.
- Every yoke and burden placed upon me as a result of satanic captivity is destroyed and lifted from now in Jesus name.

Declare Soundness of Mind, Victory over Drug Addiction and Alcoholism

- I yield my mind and spirit to the Holy Spirit of God and I refuse to be controlled by satanically projected thoughts.
- I cast down every imagination, thought, feeling and high things that exalt themselves against the knowledge of God in my life.
- I bind satanic schemes, wiles, traps, snares, innuendos, accusations, gossips, backbiting and plans against my life, family and church members.
- I bind and cut off every familiar and generational evil spirit assigned to spy on me and spoil their plans against my life in Jesus name.
- The Spirit of God gives me power, strength, sound mind, clarity, focus, vision and purpose.
- I am not confused and distracted but set my face as a flint into your desires for my life, family and church members in Jesus name. The Lord guides me with His eyes.
- Let every ungodly appetite in me for substance abuse be destroyed by the Holy Spirit in Jesus name.
- I command every trace of drugs or alcohol in my blood to be drained out in metabolism in Jesus name.
- Let the Holy Spirit destroy every substance that is defiling the temple of God in me.
- God keeps me in perfect peace because my mind is stayed on Him.
- I bind every voice of evil spirits tempting me to go back to alcohol or drugs and I reject every satanic spirit that is staging a come back into my life in Jesus name.
- I plead the blood of Jesus over my spirit, soul, body and dwellings in Jesus name.
- I cast down and pull down every stronghold, imaginations and bring into captivity every thought that exalts itself against the knowledge of God in Jesus name.
- I am not high on drugs but high on the Most High God in Jesus name.

- Let the Holy Spirit re-create every organ, receptor, neuron and nerve endings that has been affected and destroyed by drugs or alcohol in my body in Jesus name.
- Jesus Christ in me is the hope of glory and I am filled with the Holy Spirit in Jesus name.
- I have the life of God flowing through my veins, arteries and DNA in Jesus name and I am more than a conqueror.

Victory over the Spirits of
Depression and Suicide

- I bind and cast out the spirit of depression from my life in Jesus name.
- Depression cannot have dominion over me because it has been nailed to the cross of Calvary.
- I overcome the spirit of depression with the blood of Jesus and the words of God in my mouth.
- I refuse to be influenced by the spirit of depression in Jesus name.
- Every thought, imaginations and strongholds of depression in my system is cast down, pulled down and taken captive in the name of Jesus Christ the Son of God.
- I overcome depression with praise in my mouth and the two-edged sword of the word of God in my mouth in Jesus name.
- I praise God for surrounding me with His angels and filling me with His Holy Spirit in Jesus name.
- I refuse to listen to the voice of a stranger in Jesus name.
- Eternal life with God and long life on earth is my portion in Jesus name.
- I refuse to act on any strange words or voices assigned against me in Jesus name.
- I shut my ears from the voice of Satan and his cohorts and apply the blood of Jesus upon my ear gates, eye gates, touch gates, feelings gate, soul gates and spiritual gates in Jesus name.
- I condemn every tongue of devils and enemies rising in judgment against me in Jesus name.
- I refuse to be overtaken by the lips of talkers because God hides me in the secret of His tabernacle from the strife of tongues.
- I destroy every point of contact with satanic spirits in Jesus name.
- I bind the spirit of fear, discouragement and low self-esteem in Jesus name.
- I bind every lie of Satan and his cohorts against my life and destiny in Jesus name.
- The Lord has caused me to triumph always over the powers of darkness in Jesus name.
- The Lord has not given to me the spirit of fear and intimidation but the spirit of power, love and a sound mind.

- My spirit is strong, my mind is unpolluted, my emotions are sound and my will is resolute to stand on God's word until my victory manifests in Jesus name.
- I refuse to compromise my Christian values and I make up my mind to believe and do God's word in Jesus name.
- I think on things that are pure, clean, lovely, good, true, honest, of good report and virtue in Jesus name.
- I refuse to be anxious but bind the spirit of anxiety in Jesus name.
- Greater is He that is me than he that is in the world.
- I refuse to quit or give up on the Lord in Jesus name.
- I bind the spirits of suicide and cast them out from my life and presence in Jesus name.
- I shall not die but live to declare the works of God. Long life is my portion in Jesus name.
- I must not take my life because I am not mine own. God has made me fearfully and wonderfully for His purpose.
- I overcome the spirit of death by the blood of Jesus and the word of God that says, 'Death is swallowed in Victory.'
- I refuse to be stung by death because God has made me to live my life in full.
- I command the spirit of untimely death and suicide to disappear from my presence in Jesus name.
- Let God arise and let all my enemies including satanic spirits flee and be scattered seven ways.
- Mine eyes must live to see the goodness of God upon my life in the land of the living in Jesus name.
- I come boldly to the throne of grace to obtain mercy and grace to help in my time of need in Jesus name.
- I declare that I am the righteousness of God in Christ.
- I am a royal priest hood.
- I am a peculiar person.
- I am special in the eyes of God.
- I am God's battle axe
- I am more than a conqueror.
- I am victorious and triumphant in Jesus Christ over death, hell and the grave.
- I am God's ambassador on earth.
- I am a co-labourer with God.

- I am God's workmanship created in Christ Jesus.
- I am sitting in heavenly places with Jesus Christ.
- Jesus has paid the price for every trial I go through and it is already finished in Jesus name.
- I am blessed.
- The joy of the Lord is my strength.

Victory over Satanic Principalities and Powers

- I come against terrors by night, arrows that fly in the day time and pestilences or diseases that move in darkness in Jesus name.
- A thousand satanic angels and demons shall fall on my side and more than ten thousand on my right hand side.
- I trample upon spiritual lions, adders, young lions, dragons, adders, vipers, fiery serpents, crooked serpents, leviathan, bears, leopards, dogs, cats, green snakes, bondwoman, mammon and beastly animalistic devils.
- The angels of the Almighty God that excel in strength defend me always from these devils and none of them can do me any harm because I am the apple of God's eye.
- I command every satanic principality and power to bow in the name of Jesus Christ who is the head of all principalities and powers
- I pull down strongholds, imaginations and everything projected by satanic hosts against my spirit, mind, will, emotions and physical body in Jesus name.
- I reject every plan to make me a prey of the terrible and captive of the mighty in Jesus name.
- I return every dart, arrow, projection, charm, enchantment, divination, spells and sorcery against my life in Jesus name.
- No principality, power, spiritual wickedness, prince of darkness or fallen angel shall be able to persuade or dissuade me from the love of God in Jesus name.
- I declare that I am more than a conqueror, triumphant and victorious over every satanic principality through Jesus Christ my Lord and Saviour.
- Every agent of untimely death assigned against my life and family is swallowed up in victory in Jesus name.

Victory over Spiritual Storms

- I speak peace against every satanic whirlwinds, storms, tornadoes and hurricanes assigned against my life and progress in Jesus name.
- I refuse to be drowned by every flood assigned against me in Jesus name.
- The Lord makes every trial a stepping stone to higher heights in my destiny and He works all things together for my good because I love God and called according to His purpose.
- The Lord covers my head in the day of battle.
- The Lord shall always prevent my feet from been taken by sudden death.
- I am delivered from every satanic sneak attacks and uprisings in Jesus.
- I bind and blindfold every accident causing satanic spirits of wickedness, arson, murder and burglary in Jesus name.
- I return to the senders every wind of affliction assigned to destabilize me in my career, family and spiritual life in Jesus name.
- I shall not be moved or flattened by any wind, storm, rain, whirlwind, tornado or hurricane in Jesus name.

Victory over the Spirit of Untimely Death

- I take authority and dominion over every satanic mourning procession hatched in the spirit world and I command it to scatter in Jesus name. I call fire upon every mourning garment and I declare that there shall be no manifestation of Satan's intention of untimely death for me, my wife, my children, my family, friends and acquaintances in Jesus name.
- I declare that death is swallowed up in victory and I replace death with strength, vitality, mental alertness, divine health and long life in Jesus name.
- The Lord covers my head in the day of battle and prevents my feet from been taken by sudden death.
- Every stone, snare, trap, gin or weapon fashioned against me shall not prosper in Jesus name.
- Let God arise and let my enemies be scattered in seven ways.
- They that dig graves for me or any member of my family shall stumble and fall.
- I leap over every grave, wall, traps, entanglements and run through every troop assigned against my life in Jesus name.
- The Lord causes me to triumph always through our Lord Jesus Christ because greater is He that is me than he that is in the world and I am more than a conqueror.
- Because God is for me, with me and in me, no one can prosper against me in Jesus name.
- Because the Lord is my light and salvation I shall not fear what the wicked, my enemies and foes shall do unto me.
- I trample upon every serpent, scorpion, adder, vipers, leviathan, crooked serpent, fiery serpent, leopard, bear and blood sucking devils in Jesus name. I command every death causing evil spirits to bow and disappear in the name of Jesus.
- Every wicked, enemy or foe assigned to eat my flesh shall all stumble, fall and return with scattered teeth and jaws in Jesus name.
- I command the jaws of the enemies assigned against me to be locked up in Jesus name.

- Though a host or army may surround me, my heart will not fear but be confident in Jesus name.
- I call the fire of the Holy Spirit and the blood of Jesus upon every satanic paraphernalia used to invoke my spirit for harm and untimely death in Jesus name.
- A thousand shall fall on my side and ten thousand shall fall on my right side and it shall not come near me in Jesus name.
- The spirit of death cannot get me down because I am covered by the blood of Jesus Christ, therefore every angel of death must pass over my life, body, soul, spirit, dwelling, vehicle and presence.
- I reject the spirit of death, refuse to die, cannot die, will not die and shall not die because eternal life flows in my blood, veins, arteries, organs, muscles, bones, hormones and body fluids in Jesus name.
- Nothing shall move me from the place of fellowship and relationship with God.
- There is no going back on God's plans, purposes and desires for my life because I am covenanted with the greatest and richest God of heaven, earth and the universe. I shall not die but live to declare the works of God.
- I shall wait all the days of my life until my change comes in Jesus name.
- Father extend my years on earth to finish my assignment because the dead cannot praise you or serve you on earth.
- My life is hidden with Christ in God and I dwell under the shadow of the Almighty God Jehovah.
- Thank you Lord for redeeming my life from destruction and crowning me with tender mercies and loving kindness in Jesus name.
- The Lord is my length of days and the stability of my times.

Deliverance from Friendly Enemies

- Lord deliver me from strange acquaintances and enemy friends whose mouth speak vanity, and whose right hand is a right hand of falsehood in Jesus name.
- I neutralize and paralyze the spirits of envy, jealousy, lies and hatred projected from every guide, acquaintance and equals against my life. I bind every satanic advantage as a result of their negative words spoken against me in Jesus name.
- I bind the spirit of deception and double-face assigned against my friends in Jesus name.
- Let the Holy Spirit expose the wiles and snares of every secret enemy pretending to be my friend or helper in Jesus name.
- Lord, I pray for wisdom and revelation to handle friendly enemies who transform and take on the spirit of Judas Iscariot to betray me for filthy lucre in Jesus name.
- I bind every spirit of vacillation assigned against my friends in my time of testing in Jesus name.
- I shield my friends, family and acquaintances with the blood of Jesus from every satanic influence to attack or come against me in Jesus name
- All enemy friends, foes and wicked who desire my failure or calamity shall live to see my justification, glorification, testimonies and triumph in Jesus name.
- I bind the spirit of disillusionment assigned against me as a result of friendly fire or friendly disappointment in Jesus name.
- I cast out and reject every parasitic relationships and replace them with symbiotic ones in Jesus name.
- I bind every friendly schemes, innuendos, manipulations, wiles, craftiness, maligning, back stabbing, backbiting and gossips in Jesus name.
- Let God reveal the hearts of my friends like Jesus Christ knew the hearts of men and committed Himself to none in Jesus name.
- I declare that my friends shall be a blessing to me in Jesus name.
- I thank God for Jesus Christ who is my friend that sticks closer to me than earthly friends and relatives.
- I put my hope on Jesus Christ who is the Rock upon which I stand.

Declare who you are in Christ

- I am the righteousness of God in Christ.
- I am a chosen generation.
- I am redeemed by the blood of Jesus
- I am seated with Jesus in heavenly places.
- I am blessed with every spiritual blessing in heavenly places in Jesus Christ.
- I am destined to win, empowered to succeed and armed to overcome Satan, every dart, arrows or issues thrown against me.
- I am sealed with the Holy Spirit of God until the redemption of the purchased possession.
- I have been translated from the kingdom of darkness into the kingdom of Jesus Christ.
- The Greater one, Jesus Christ dwells in me.
- I am heaven's diplomat on earth, a citizen of heaven and an ambassador of Jesus Christ.
- I am royal priest of God.
- I am a peculiar person.
- I am God's battle axe.
- I am joint heir with Jesus Christ.
- I am triumphant over the issues of life in Jesus name.
- I am sanctified and filled with wisdom.
- I am born again of the incorruptible seed.
- I am pressing forward towards the mark of the prize of God's high calling for my life.
- I am more than a conqueror.

Victory over the Spirit of Poverty

- I bind the spirit of poverty and reject poverty in my life, family and ministry in the name of Jesus.
- I destroy the cycles and generational curse of poverty against my life and family in Jesus name.
- I am blessed by God to be a blessing to others and to the poor in Jesus name.
- I declare that I shall contribute to the reduction of poverty statistics on earth in Jesus name.
- My light is shining out of obscurity in Jesus name.
- I reject slackness of hands, laziness and procrastination that causes poverty in Jesus name.
- I shall not live a life of borrowing but shall be transformed to become a lender to many in Jesus name.
- I am a joint heir with God, Jesus Christ and the Holy Spirit.
- The grace of God through Jesus Christ who was made poor that I might become rich is upon my life.
- I am triumphant over all financial battles, challenges and issues of life in Jesus name.
- Because I am redeemed by the blood of Jesus Christ, I suffer no loses in my life and in everything I do.
- I am profitable because the Lord teaches me to make profit and gives me power to get wealth.
- I possess the gates of my enemies and the Lord is enlarging my territories of financial influence in Jesus name.
- I possess the promise of God in a land flowing with milk and honey in Jesus name
- The Lord is my help in a strong city in Jesus name.
- The Lord satisfies me abundantly in the time of famine.
- I overcome the wiles and pressures of the black horse man of economic depression and economic woes in Jesus name.

Victory in a Depressed Economy

- I shall be satisfied in the days of famine and economic depression.
- I shall not retrogress in the time of depression but have divine advantage to rise above every economic storm in Jesus name.
- I bind the spirit of the black horseman assigned to cause economic hardship in my life and area of financial activity in Jesus name.
- I bind and cast out every Philistine spirit assigned to cover my spiritual and physical wells of income with sand in Jesus name.
- The Lord has provided a brook Cherith for my sustenance during famine.
- I refuse to be discouraged by rumours of depression, bills and financial crunch in Jesus name.
- I declare that all my needs shall be met even in a time of national and global austerity in Jesus name.
- I thank God for financial prudence and increased income during economic depression in Jesus name.
- I thank God for open heavens and rain upon my land and areas of influence, business and ministry in Jesus name.
- I thank God for the spirit of entrepreneurship on Joseph and Isaac in Jesus name.
- I release the ability for supernatural multiplication and finding wealth that was on Jesus Christ upon my life.
- I am not anxious for daily sustenance of my life, business and ministry in Jesus name.
- I take authority and dominion and cast out every evil spirit responsible for famine, austerity, drought and suffering in Jesus name.
- I thank God for providing a Goshen for me in time of economic depression.
- Every shaking of economies by God shall release the glory of God upon my life and business in Jesus name.
- I uncover every well and dig more wells of life and streams of income in Jesus name.
- I am profitable to my generation and I shall contribute significantly to the advancement of humanity in Jesus name.
- I claim new territories in the time of famine and economic depression in Jesus name.

Proclaim your Blessings in
Jesus Christ

- I am blessed going out and coming in.
- I am blessed in the city.
- Blessed in my job.
- Blessed in my business.
- Blessed in my shop.
- Blessed in my internet business.
- Blessed in everything I lay my hands to do.
- I initiate, continue and perpetrate a generation of blessed family, blessed people, blessed business and blessed ministry.
- The Lord shall open his good treasure, the heaven to give the rain upon everything I do and bless every work of my hand.
- I shall lend and give to many people and I shall not live a life of borrowing or perpetual borrowing.
- I command the treasures of darkness and riches of secret places to abound towards me and answer to my name.
- The Lord loads me with benefits daily and supplies all my need according to his riches in glory by Christ Jesus.
- I shall drink from wellsprings of life, eat from vineyards I did not plant and dwell in goodly houses in Jesus name.
- I claim spiritual, psychological and physical financial territories.
- I am blessed and kept by the power of God.
- God's face is shining on me and His grace abounds towards me.
- God's countenance is upon me and He gives me peace.
- The rock is pouring oil upon my path.
- My lines are fallen on pleasant places because I have a good heritage in the Lord.
- The Lord is the portion of my inheritance, my cup and He maintains my lot in the land of the living.
- Every spiritual, social, governmental, national, international, intercontinental, economic and legal territory that belongs to me is enlarging supernaturally.
- I call forth people from every tongue, tribe, nation and race whom God has assigned to favour me and be a blessing to my destiny.
- The blessings of God upon my life would make me richer and would not add sorrow to it.

- I shall eat every fruit of my labour in the name of Jesus.
- I shall not sow or plant and another eat every fruit of my labour.
- Every negative circumstance in my life must turn around for my good in Jesus name.
- I am an employment provider and distributor of heaven's abundance to others
- I am blessed by God to be a blessing to others and the poor.
- I operate in godly excellence, wisdom, knowledge, understanding, efficiency, effectiveness and humility.
- I operate in new realms and dimensions of kingdom glory and power.

Prayer for Supernaturally Assisted Project Completion

- I declare in the name of Jesus that every project in my life shall be completed supernaturally in Jesus name.
- The zeal of the Lord shall consume my heart in every project I embark upon.
- Jesus the author and finisher of my faith shall supernaturally assist me in completion of every assignment, project and businesses he has desired for me.
- No weapons formed against my projects and businesses shall prosper in Jesus name.
- I bind the spirit of the antichrist, red dragon, mammon, mystery Babylon, Jezebel and Belial assigned against my life, projects and businesses in Jesus name.
- I receive the anointing, strength, tenacity, focus required for completion in Jesus name.
- I receive the finishing anointing from God and His Son Jesus Christ who is the Alpha and Omega, Beginning and the End, The Amen of all things and destinies!
- Because Jesus said, 'it is finished,' I decree that everything I lay my hands to do by the unction of the Holy Spirit must be finished in Jesus name.
- I bind the spirits of Tobias, Sanballat and Gesem assigned to discourage me from completing my projects in Jesus name.
- I bind the spirit of procrastination, delay, postponement, lethargy, body weakness, fear and lack of ambition assigned against my projects and businesses in Jesus name.
- I bind every satanic spirit of abortion and near completion in Jesus name.
- Every plan of God for my life shall be completed, fulfilled and achieved by the power of God in Jesus name.
- He that began a good work in me shall complete it in Jesus name.
- I thank God because His thoughts towards me are thoughts of peace and not evil and He would give me the expected end of my heart desire in Jesus name.
- I bind every spirit of unfinished projects or assignments in Jesus name.

- I come against the spoiler of destinies and scatter the horns of every beast pushing against my efforts in Jesus name.
- I receive power to travail and deliver the plans and purposes of God for my life in Jesus name.
- I shall not begin a project without finishing, I shall not go on a journey without returning. I shall not pursue without overtaking, I shall not lay foundation without completing the building, and I shall not call without receiving an answer from God in Jesus name.
- I refuse to be hindered by hurts, lack of forgiveness and resentments and therefore release everyone who has offended me and pray for release by anyone I have offended in Jesus name.
- I cut off and destroy every satanic snare on my journey to the finishing line of victory and triumph in Jesus name.
- I press toward the mark of the prize of the high calling of God in Jesus name.

Proclaim your Victory over
Financial and Mineral Kingdoms

- I call forth every currency on earth to enhance the fulfilment of my destiny in Jesus name.
- I call forth British pounds, U.S.Dollars, Canadian Dollars, Euros, Yen, Naira, Rands, Ghanaian Dollars, Rupees, Deutschmark, French Francs and as many as the Lord pleases into my bank accounts.
- I shall benefit from every mineral resource that is my portion on earth in Jesus name because I am a joint heir with Jesus Christ and God.
- I wash my steps in butter and the rock is pouring out oil in my path in Jesus name.
- Like Asher the son of Jacob, I deep my feet in spiritual, psychological and physical oils in Jesus name.

Prayer for Success in Exams

- I thank God who makes me to triumph always and gives me victory and success in everything I do.
- I release the spirit of wisdom and revelation in the knowledge of God and the things He has created for me to study and understand in Jesus name.
- I receive knowledge for wisdom, instruction, perception, justice, judgment and equity through the Holy Spirit in Jesus name.
- I thank God for a strategic study plan to cover every subject of examination in Jesus name.
- I shall read, hear and increase learning in Jesus name.
- Like Daniel I ask God to give me knowledge and skill in all learning in Jesus name.
- I shall study to show myself approved of God a workman that does not need to be ashamed and rightly dividing the word of truth in Jesus name.
- I declare that God has given me the tongue of the learned to know what to answer during my examinations in Jesus name.
- I shall receive supernatural wisdom in areas I have not studied as the Jews said of Jesus, 'How knoweth this man letters having never learned?'
- I decree according to Proverbs 15:28 that my heart shall study to answer because I am the righteousness of God in Christ.
- I shall excel in my studies because the fear of God is the beginning of wisdom, knowledge and understanding.
- I receive wisdom from God and excel over my colleagues because wisdom is the principal thing.
- I thank God for revelation, accuracy and sharp shooting in my studies and preparations for examinations in Jesus name.
- I bind every spirit of failure, body weakness, infirmity and fear in Jesus name.
- I declare that my brain and mind is not porous, forgetful, and hard of hearing or learning in Jesus name.
- I come against cycles of satanic attacks during my examinations and replace them with new cycles of spiritual, psychological and physical alertness in Jesus name.

- I thank God for the Spirit of God in me that gives me an excellent spirit, knowledge, understanding, interpretation of dreams, showing hard sentences and dissolving of doubts as was found in Daniel.
- I excel above my fellows in every examination in Jesus name because the Lord has made me the head and not the tail.
- I shall not fail any examinations because the Spirit of God in me is my teacher, counsellor and gives me wisdom and insight for witty ideas and inventions in Jesus name.
- The enemy shall not gainsay or miss-interpret my ideas, solutions and answers in Jesus name.
- My hand writing shall be legible and clear before those marking my papers in Jesus name.
- I cover every examiner that is assigned to mark my papers with the blood of Jesus Christ.
- I declare that those marking my papers shall be filled with equity, justice, fairness and kindness in Jesus name.
- I believe that I am coming out of the examinations hall with distinctions and excellence in Jesus name.
- I receive light from God who reveals deep and secret things and knows what is in the dark and makes known secret things in Jesus name.
- I reject every form of brain block, brain drain and forgetfulness in Jesus name.
- I reject failure, re-sits and repeats in my examinations in Jesus name.
- I come against negative influences and satanic oppressions and fits against those marking my papers in Jesus name.
- My papers shall not be missing or lost in Jesus name.
- I proclaim that they shall be of a sound mind and spirit in Jesus name.
- I am pressing forward to the mark of the prize of the high calling of God in Jesus name.
- I grow in stature wisdom and spiritual understanding in Jesus name.

Prayer for Life Partner

- I declare that my face and countenance shall shine before the person God intends for me in Jesus name.
- I release the favour of God upon my life in the area of marriage in Jesus name.
- My lines shall fall on pleasant places concerning my desire to get married.
- I shall not be blindfolded spiritually from the person God intends for me in Jesus name.
- I declare that there shall be no procrastinators or time wasters in my path way in Jesus name.
- I shall spiritually locate and be located by my perfect life partner in Jesus name.
- I bind, scatter and cast out every generational curses, characteristics and cycles of a lifetime of singleness and loneliness in my family line in Jesus name.
- I take authority, dominion and neutralize, paralyze, bind and cast out every satanic covenant, human covenants, and soul ties made knowingly or unknowingly in my past in Jesus name.
- I receive favour to be find and be found amongst millions of single believers on earth in Jesus name.
- I am set free because of the most powerful covenant I have with Jesus Christ through His blood.
- The blood of Jesus sets me free from every curse of the law against my life and family.
- I declare that I shall be married and settled in my own family home in Jesus name.

Bind every Negative Seed
In Courtship

- I prophesy that my courtship shall begin very shortly in Jesus name.
- I declare and proclaim that my courtship shall not be very long in Jesus name.
- My courtship shall be filled with sanctity and holiness in Jesus name
- There shall be no wrong seeds of sexual sin, abuse and violence in my courtship in Jesus name.
- I bind every voice or spiritual persuasions of negativity against my courtship in Jesus name.
- I nullify every spell, charm, incantations and curses assigned against my courtship in Jesus name.
- We receive strength to overcome every temptation and trial during our courtship in Jesus name.
- We overcome every fiery dart of Satan and his cohorts against our courtship, wedding and marriage in Jesus name.
- My courtship shall be a time of prayers, godly counselling, adjustments and preparation for the wedding.
- I declare that our courtship period shall be filled with the wisdom and fear of God in Jesus name.
- We bind every negative seed of gossip, backbiting, slander, traps, snares and wiles of satanic spirits and agents of Satan in Jesus name.

Victory over Enemies of Courtship

- I bind every enemy of my courtship and marriage in Jesus name
- I come against every secret plan of acquaintances who are not happy about my courtship.
- Let the Holy Spirit expose them in Jesus name.
- They shall live to see my wedding and marriage in Jesus name.
- I am spiritually alert in time of my courtship to receive divine unction, inspiration and revelation against every wile of Satan in Jesus name.
- I send the fire of the Holy Ghost on every satanic points of contact, charms and satanic paraphernalia that shall be presented to me as gift during my wedding in Jesus name
- My future life partner shall not be bewitched, charmed or deceived against our plans to get married in Jesus name.
- Our marriage shall not be part of the divorce statistics in Jesus name.
- Satan shall not be able to use our relatives against our relationship in Jesus name.
- Our marriage shall not be barren but abundantly blessed, fruitful in all areas of life, abound in grace, favour, unconditional love and marital bliss in Jesus name
- Our children shall be blessed and God fearing in Jesus name.
- Our family shall contribute immensely and positively to the growth of the body of Christ and our community and world in Jesus name.
- I proclaim supernatural supply for courtship, wedding and marriage.
- We shall not lack finances, help, support and favour as we prepare for the wedding and marriage in Jesus name.
- The Lord shall supply all our need according to his riches in Christ Jesus.
- The Lord shall give us wisdom to handle every phase of marriage, child birth, child upbringing, streams of income, neighbours and relationships in Jesus name.
- Our family shall be like heaven on earth in Jesus name.

Victory over the Spirit of Divorce

- I bind every evil spirit of strife, misunderstanding, suspicion, fear, and intimidation, lack of communication, nagging, manipulation, oppression and abuse assigned against my spouse and me in Jesus name.
- I uproot and throw down every seed and initiation of divorce in Jesus name.
- I refuse to be caught in the web of strife, quarrel and misunderstanding that leads to divorce in Jesus name.
- I set myself free from every spiritual and physical divorce case in Jesus name.
- My marriage shall not end up in divorce in Jesus name because the Lord hates divorce.
- I pray for wisdom to handle my spouse in Jesus name.
- I call back my spouse into our marriage in Jesus name.
- I bind and cast out the spirit of the strange woman (man) interfering with my marriage in Jesus name.
- I bind and cast out every spirit of Jezebel interfering with our marriage in Jesus name.
- I declare that our separation is temporary and God shall cause our separation to bring sober reflections and desire for reconciliation in Jesus name.
- I release the spirit of forgiveness, the fruit of temperance and longsuffering in our relationship in Jesus name.
- I declare that no man, woman or devil shall be able to separate our marriage because it was joined together by God in Jesus name.
- I bind every blindfolding evil spirit in Jesus name.
- I take authority and complete dominion over the spirit of pride, self and ego in Jesus name.
- I release clarity of spiritual vision and the mission of our marriage into our relationship in Jesus name.
- I release marital bliss, mutual understanding, mutual respect, agape love and forgiveness into our marriage in Jesus name.
- I thank God for restoring the love fire and fervency for one another (stronger than we first met each other) in Jesus name.

Declare Family Fruitfulness In
Your Marriage

- We are as fruitful as the vine in every area of our relationship and barrenness is not our portion in Jesus name.
- We are fruitful in the fruit of our body and nothing is barren in our lives in Jesus name
- We bind the spirit of abortion and declare that nothing shall cast our young in Jesus name.
- We destroy every satanic covenant of barrenness in our lives made knowingly or unknowingly in Jesus name.
- We bind satanic spiritual husbands and wives fighting against our fruitfulness and destroy every covenant made with them in Jesus name.
- We destroy every soul tie and covenants with past sexual acquaintances and friends in Jesus name.
- We shall keep house and be joyful parents of children in Jesus name.
- We take authority, bind and cast out every spirit of barrenness and abortion assigned against our lives in Jesus name.
- Let God repair any damaged organ in our bodies supernaturally by the stripes of Jesus Christ.
- We believe God for creative miracles in our body organs, systems and hormones in Jesus name.
- We declare that every area of our lives and business is fruitful in Jesus name.
- We are like trees planted by the river side whose leaves are always green, bringing forth fruit in due season and whatsoever we lay our hands to do shall prosper in Jesus name.
- We flourish as a palm tree and grow as cedar of Lebanon in Jesus name and still bring forth fruit in old age.
- I declare that our family altar is a regular place of daily spiritual communion with the Lord.
- We enjoy agape love and submission in our relationship in Jesus name.
- Our home is a place of marital bliss, peace and rest for divine revelation and progress in Jesus name.

Declare Victory over every Evil
Assignment against your Family

- We bind and cast out every spirit of jezebel, strange women, strange men, paedophiles, gangs and perverts assigned against our home in Jesus name.
- God gives his angels charge over us and places the edge of protection around our home by day and night.
- No plague and calamity shall come near our dwelling in Jesus name.
- Our home shall not be broken into nor ravaged by fire in Jesus name.
- We bind and cast out the evil spirits of the age, strife, misunderstanding, separation, violence and divorce assigned against our family in Jesus name.
- Every satanic principalities, agents or witches in our region of abode must cease to operate because of our presence and prayers in Jesus name.
- No satanic agents shall be able to penetrate our windows, walls, roof and doors in Jesus name.
- When Satan and his cohorts shall see the blood of Jesus over our home they shall pass over in Jesus name.

Proclaim Family Blessings

- I declare and decree that my wife (husband), children and family are blessed in Jesus name.
- My children are taught of the Lord and great is their peace.
- The children that the Lord has given or shall give to me are meant for signs and wonders.
- Our children live in obedience and submission to the plan of God
- I declare that the unconditional love of God flows in our family relationship in Jesus name.
- I cover our home, appliances, equipment, computers, telecommunications, amenities and facilities with the blood of Jesus.
- Every bill and mortgages shall be paid before due term in Jesus name and our home shall not be repossessed.
- Our family is blessed with finances and many streams of income and we shall lack no food, clothing, household materials, electronics and finances to help others.

Call Forth your Streams of Income

- The heavens are open to us because we are tithe payers and givers to our local church and charity.
- Therefore, we receive unction due to open heavens for many streams of financial income in Jesus name.
- We are like trees planted by rivers of water. We bring forth fruit in His season and our leaves shall not wither. Whatsoever we lay our hands to do shall prosper in Jesus name.
- We receive income from any of the following in Jesus name: transportation, auto sales and repair services, fast food shops and restaurants, airline services and booking agents, gymnasium, bed and breakfast, professional sports and football, Internet trade, internet café, IT, stocks and shares, government bonds, goods market, precious minerals, petroleum, natural gas, fertilizers, plank and treated wood, financial market, ISA, mutual funds, high interest deposits, collectors' items, intellectual properties, real estate, buy-to-let, off plan sales, property redevelopment, educational services, commodities, agriculture, animal husbandry, poultry, hides & skin, milk and wool production, Jewels and Jewelries conglomerates companies chain department stores, shops, syndications and mergers expert, politics, work from home, fashion, perfumery, toiletries, pharmaceuticals, import and export, currencies, education, handy man, contractor, web designer, graphic artists, furniture, legal services, immigration services, welfare and caring services, florist, broadcasting, engineering, sports, acting, cleaning services, child minding, barbing, hairdressing, green energy, gardening, sales and marketing, seminar and conferences organization, transportation, cab and limo services, catering services, holidays and recreational services, halls for hire, etc. in Jesus name.

Dedicate your House Or Flat
To God

- I dedicate this house to God Almighty, Jehovah, Jesus Christ and the Holy Spirit.
- I apply the blood of Jesus on the foundation, walls, doors, windows, roof, ceiling, lounge, bedrooms, kitchen, stores, garden, shed, furniture, utensils, appliances and every other thing in Jesus name.
- I bind, root out and cast out every contrary spirit that is dwelling or has dwelt in this house perpetrating divorce, suicide, sexual perversion, strife, violence, fear, accidents, alcoholism, drug addiction, prostitution, depression, assassinations, duping, infirmities, repossessions, generational curses, burglary, fire and untimely death in Jesus name.
- I make this house uncomfortable for every satanic spirit with the fire of the Holy Spirit and the blood of Jesus. I command all of you to go to the dry places in Jesus name.
- I bind all the principalities, powers, rulers of darkness, spiritual wickedness in high places and witches that control and manipulate the people in this street, area, borough and city. I plead the blood of Jesus over my region of abode.
- The blood of Jesus on the entry points of this house prevents every death, plague and calamity causing spirits.
- Every visitor, relatives, friends, neighbours and acquaintances who enter this house shall bring joy, peace and blessings instead of evil, strife, gossip, evil report or bad news.
- This house shall not be affected by extreme weather conditions and natural disasters like whirlwinds, tornadoes, hurricanes, floods, earthquakes in Jesus name.
- I declare that this house is Bethel, the house of God and mount Zion where there is a flow of angelic host from heaven to earth bringing revelation, unction, anointing, resources, protection, deliverance, favour and peace in Jesus name.
- This abode is a peaceable habitation, a sure and quiet resting place in Jesus name.

Declare your Business Breakthrough and Increase

- Every business I lay my hands on shall prosper and be profitable in Jesus name.
- I bind every evil spirit assigned to hinder the progress of my business.
- Because I am a tithe paying child of God, the spirit of mammon and devourer shall not affect my business.
- The Lord rebukes and I also rebuke every devourer assigned to grind my business to a halt.
- I shall not be blindfolded spiritually from discerning crooks, dupes, parasites, lazy applicants and embezzlers in Jesus name.
- The Lord gives me wisdom to operate my business for profitability and service to humanity in Jesus name.
- I bind and cast out every spirit of fear preventing me from taking calculated and Holy Spirit directed risks in Jesus name.
- I launch out into the deep and I use every storm in business as a stepping stone in Jesus name.
- The Lord shall continue to show me my multiple streams of income as my business progresses in Jesus name.
- I declare that everyone who partners with me shall enhance my business and make it grow and profitable in Jesus name.
- The Lord shall give me wisdom to employ the best staff at every phase of my business in Jesus name.
- I bind and cast out the spirits of compromise in business in Jesus name.
- My business shall find favour in the sight of the Lord, government organizations, conglomerate companies, city boroughs, men and women in Jesus name.
- Strangers and people from all races, tribes, tongues and nations shall be a blessing to me and enhance the profitability of my business in Jesus name.
- I prophesy to the four winds of the earth to blow on every dry bone of my business and I speak strength to every weak area and I command them to begin to arise, grow and expand in Jesus name.
- I call forth customers and contracts into my business from the four corners of the earth and the seven continents in Jesus name.

- I ask God to release business acumen, organization, excellence, efficiency, effectiveness, stability, consistency, orderliness, timeliness, accuracy, patience, diligence, wisdom, understanding, the fear of the Lord, charity, customer delight into my business in Jesus name.
- I prophesy that my business holdings shall turnover and make profits in millions and billions of currencies in Jesus name because the Lord teaches me to make profit.
- The Lord shall open His good treasure and command the rain to fall on every area of my business in Jesus name.
- I shall be a market leader in my area of business because the Lord says, 'I shall be the head and not the tail in Jesus name.'
- My business is blessed in the city, in the field, in the state, in the country, internationally and globally in Jesus name.
- I receive every power and anointing from God Almighty to prosper and be in health even as my soul prospers in Jesus name.
- I ask God to bless me indeed and enlarge my territory of business and influence in Jesus name.
- I decree that no witch, wizard, occultist, enchanter, sorcerer, prognosticator, diviners or any satanic agent shall be able to close down my business because it is dedicated to the Lord and covered by the blood of Jesus.
- I paralyze the effect of charms and spells against my business holdings and I reject litigations and law suits against my business in Jesus name.
- The Lord is opening my eyes to see business opportunities and breakthrough ideas in Jesus name.
- Like a little mustard seed cast into the ground which grows into a mighty tree, so shall my business holdings grow in Jesus name.

Prayer for Divine Protection

- I declare that I am far from oppression and fear in Jesus name.
- No weapon formed against me shall prosper in Jesus name.
- I am safe under the shadow of the Almighty God because I dwell in His secret place of fellowship and communion in Jesus name.
- I am not afraid for the terror by night nor arrows that fly during the day time.
- Every pestilence and disease that walk in darkness shall not come near me or my dwelling. And I reject every spirit of infirmity in Jesus name.
- I confess, declare and decree that the Lord is my refuge and fortress and in Him I always put my trust.
- I am not afraid of the snare of the fowler or noisome pestilence because God covers me with His feathers and under His wings I trust.
- God has given His angels charge over me and I shall not fall, stumble nor dash my feet against any stone in Jesus name.
- Almighty God Jehovah Gibbor fights my battles and He prepares a table before me in the presence of my enemies.
- No witch, wizard, satanic assignment shall be able to oppress me during my sleep because I am covered by the blood of Jesus and protected by the angels of God in Jesus name.
- God has prepared a table before me in the presence of my enemies and He has anointed my head with oil making my cup to overflow.
- Goodness and mercy follow me all the days of my life and I shall dwell in the house of God forever.
- I trample upon every lion and adder, young lions, lions, dragons, antichrist, the leopard, bear, fiery serpent, crooked serpent and leviathan in Jesus name.
- The Lord protects me with a wall of fire, robe of righteousness, the blood of Jesus and His holy angels in Jesus name.
- I am divinely insured against calamity accident and untimely death in Jesus name.
- I thank God for journey mercies and divine protection as I travel on land by car, bus, trucks, jeep or by boat, ocean liner, cruise boat, ship, aircraft, helicopter, hovercraft, speed boat, cable car or tour vans.

- I cover my vehicle, aircraft, helicopter, hovercraft or cable car with the blood of Jesus and I bind and nullify every covenant with death in Jesus name.
- My presence repels every diabolical and satanic influence against my vehicle, aircraft or boat in Jesus name.
- My presence brings safety to my vehicle, aircraft or boat in Jesus name.
- I come against storms, hurricanes, tornadoes, bad weather and mid-air collisions in Jesus name.
- I cover the drivers, pilots, co-pilots, flight engineers, air hostesses of my aircraft, vehicle or hovercraft with the blood of Jesus.
- I take complete authority and dominion over every evil spirit of terrorism, plane crash, mid-air explosions and hi-jacking in Jesus name.
- I come against loss of air pressure and altitude in Jesus name.
- My aircraft shall take off safely and land safely without skidding or missing the tarmac in Jesus name.
- The Lord shall bless and keep my going out and my coming home in Jesus name.
- I reject every error from the control tower in direction of my aircraft in Jesus name.
- I cover every engine of my aircraft with the blood of Jesus and declare that there shall be no engine failure in Jesus name.
- I shall not enter any vehicle, aircraft or boat that is doomed for calamity in Jesus name because the Lord orders my steps and I shall here a voice behind me, 'this is the way walk ye in it.'
- I thank God for divine protection wherever I lodge or sleep in Jesus name.

Prayer Declarations for Interviews and Employment

- I thank God for divine favour for supernatural employment opportunities in Jesus name.
- I shall not tarry long in seeking a new Job because God grants me grace and favour in the sight of employers in Jesus name.
- I declare that My God shall turn the hearts of employers, chairmen, directors and CEOs to favour me during my employment interview in Jesus name.
- I thank God for the appropriate employment opportunity for this season in Jesus name.
- I receive supernatural unction to answer interview questions in Jesus name.
- The Lord shall give to me divine wisdom, utterance and boldness during my job interviews in Jesus name.
- I bind the spirit of fear, low self esteem, intimidation, delay and doubt in Jesus name.
- I set myself free from every cycle of joblessness in Jesus name and I declare new cycles of favour, forward movement and employment in Jesus name.
- I come against racist tendencies and segregations in Jesus name.
- I declare that I shall be gainfully employed in my area of interest and talent in Jesus name.
- The Lord covers me with favour like a shield in Jesus name.
- Father, let my line fall on pleasant places in Jesus name.
- Like Joseph I shall rise up supernaturally in my place of employment and God shall use me to be a blessing to my company and employers in Jesus name.
- My promotions shall be speedy and financially rewarding in Jesus name.
- I bind every satanic spirit assigned against my new job in Jesus name.
- I bind the spirit of joblessness and declare that the Lord shall find something for my hands and brain to accomplish in Jesus name.
- I confess that I shall be a problem solver in my new job in Jesus name.

- I thank God for dethroning the servant that is riding on my horse in Jesus name.
- I take my place in the city and receive the wealth of the wicked that is meant for me in Jesus name.
- I am blessed in the city, blessed in the field, blessed in everything I lay my hands to do in Jesus name.
- I declare that the next job that the Lord shall provide for me shall be a stepping stone to my streams of income in Jesus name.

Prayers For Divine Favour

- I release the supernatural favour of God upon my life.
- God covers me with favour like a shield
- A people I do not know shall seek my favour
- Queens of Sheba and Seba shall bring gifts to me in Jesus name.
- Strangers shall serve me and feed my flock in Jesus name and as soon as they hear of me they shall obey me.
- My steps are covered with favour and breakthrough in Jesus name.
- I shall not labour for favour but I receive it by reason of my divine covenant with God Almighty and His Son Jesus Christ.
- I declare that one day of favour in my life shall overtake a thousand days of my labour in Jesus name.
- I shall reap as I plough and harvest shall meet with harvest in Jesus name.
- I thank God for the anointing for unsolicited favour and multiple blessings in Jesus name.
- I release by the power of God my new realms and new dimensions of favour and divine seasons in Jesus name.
- My face shall shine before kings, rulers, men and women because the Lord lifts His countenance upon me, makes His face to shine upon me and gives me grace and peace in Jesus name.
- I move according to God's divine leading and therefore covered by the glory cloud for breakthrough, open doors and divine momentum and progress in Jesus name.

Breakthrough Declarations for Pastors and the Five-fold Ministry

- I am victorious over every satanic spirit assigned against my ministry and church members in Jesus name.
- I am a success in ministry and not a failure in Jesus name.
- I magnify my ministry in Jesus name and hold my position in Christ with dignity and high regard.
- I am triumphant in ministry because I did not call myself or take this honour to myself.
- The Lord will equip and bless my ministry because I am a co-labourer with Him and He supplies all my ministry need according to His riches in glory by Christ Jesus.
- I am justified and glorified in Christ because of His call upon my life.
- I take complete authority and dominion over Satan and his principalities and agents over my nation, state, city, borough and street where my ministry is located in Jesus name.
- I bind and cast out the spirit of untimely death and unfinished projects in ministry in Jesus name.
- My ministry shall not fail because Jesus has declared that the gates of hell shall never prevail against the church of God.
- I refuse to be frustrated by satanic agents, governmental, council, financial and societal institutions or persons and neighbours assigned against my ministry in Jesus name.
- I rule and reign triumphant over the powers of darkness assigned against my ministry in Jesus name.
- I come against, uproot and throw down every satanic structure and systems assigned to hinder my ministry in Jesus name.
- I cover my ministry and the church of God with the blood of Jesus and shield every staff, church member and intending members in my area of operation with the blood of Jesus Christ.
- No weapon formed against my ministry and the church of God shall prosper in Jesus name.
- I declare that satanic agents assigned to pollute and mingle with staff and church members shall be exposed and flushed out in Jesus name.

- I bind, scatter and destroy every plan hatched in the witches' coven, satanic dens, groves, marine world and second heavens against my life, spouse, children and ministry in Jesus name.
- I bind every evil spirit of sexual perversion, sexual permissiveness and gradual sexual enticement assigned against me in Jesus name.
- I bind, uproot, spoil, throw down and cast out the spirit of Jezebel and her children in Jesus name.
- I come against strange men and women assigned to pollute the church of God in Jesus name.
- I release the spirit of repentance and fear of God upon my ministry and church of God in Jesus name.
- I bind every spirit of covetousness, filthy lucre and financial mismanagement in Jesus name.
- I bind and cast out every spirit assigned to pollute the call of God on my life with the love of money, sex, pride, ego and power in Jesus name.
- I declare that my spouse shall serve with me in ministry and not be a stumbling block in Jesus name.
- I cover my children and spouse with the blood of Jesus Christ and shield them in prayer from every counter attacks of Satan in Jesus name.
- I declare that those who serve with me in ministry as pastors, ministers, deacons, group leaders shall work in harmony with me in Jesus name.
- I thank God for loyal and God fearing associates in Jesus name.
- Let every manifestation of Tobias, Sanballat, Geshem, Judas Iscariot, Alexander the coppersmith, Demas, Diotrephes be exposed and dealt with in my ministry in Jesus name.
- I condemn every tongue that rise up in judgment against me, my spouse, children and ministry in Jesus name
- I refuse to be overtaken by the strife of tongues and the lips of talkers in Jesus name.
- I bind every spirit of envy and jealousy assigned against my life, family, ministry and church in Jesus name.
- I thank God for raising up intercessors against sneak attacks in my ministry and church in Jesus name.
- I shall not be blindfolded to impending trouble, calamity or satanic attack in Jesus name.

- I declare that I am mentally alert, physically strong and spiritually sensitive in Jesus name.
- I bind and cast out every scattering spirit assigned to scatter the membership and deplete church growth in Jesus name.
- I declare that my ministry shall be supported by praying members and associates in Jesus name.
- I call forth a fresh baptism of the Holy Spirit upon every church member for prayer fire and power in Jesus name.
- I bind and cast out every spirit of confusion, distraction and entanglement in Jesus name.
- I overcome and reject every evil spirit assigned to cause church fights and church splits in Jesus name.
- I ask God for wisdom to lead, minister, and govern those God has called into my ministry and Church in Jesus name.
- I call forth supernatural and natural flow of finances to meet every need in ministry in Jesus name.
- I call forth open heavens in my ministry and church as a result of faithful tithe paying members and associates in Jesus name.
- I call forth members from every walk of life, profession, tribe, tongue, nation, race into my ministry and church in Jesus name.
- I ask God for the anointing to preach, teach, heal, love and chastise those God has placed under my leadership in Jesus name.
- I declare that I shall not be a men- pleaser or respecter of persons, status, class, race or pedigree in Jesus name.
- I declare that I shall not judge by the hearing of ears or seeing of the eyes in Jesus name.
- My ministry and church is pressing forward and abounding in favour and grace of God.
- I declare that every ministerial department is being fulfilled in Jesus name.
- I thank God for expansion, enlargement of territory and finances to take the gospel to nations of the earth in Jesus name.
- I thank God for finances for technological assistance in ministry in Jesus name.
- The members of my ministry and church are blessed, filled with favour and fear of the Lord in Jesus name.
- I bind the spirit of stinginess and selfishness in my ministry and church in Jesus name.

- I release the spirit of giving, stewardship, ministry to the poor and to the community in Jesus name.
- I ask God to release His finishing and provision grace upon every building project, crusade, conferences and community projects in Jesus name.
- My ministry and church is mount Zion where there is deliverance and holiness in Jesus name.
- I thank God for proper protocol and etiquette in every area of my life, ministry and church in Jesus name.
- I thank God for the spirit of excellence, effectiveness, efficiency and diligence upon my life, ministry leaders and church in Jesus name.
- I decree and declare that I shall continue to press forward to the mark of the prize of the high calling of God in Christ Jesus.
- I thank God for making me a significant contributor to the expansion of the kingdom of God on earth in Jesus name.
- I thank God for helping me finish my assignment very well and make heaven in Jesus name

Hitch Free Pregnancy
and Delivery

- I cover this miracle of child conception, development and growth taking place in my womb with the blood of Jesus.
- I declare that every hormone, enzyme, lymphatic system, glands, adrenal glands, amniotic fluid, umbilical cord, uterus, blood system and brain control centres in my body shall positively facilitate the proper growth of the child in my womb in Jesus name.
- I pray that God's Holy Spirit shall overshadow the child in my womb for total conformity to His desired plan, destiny, purpose and physic in Jesus name.
- I declare that the child in my womb is predestined according to the foreknowledge of God to be conformed to the image of Jesus Christ who is the first born of the Church of God and is therefore called, justified and glorified.
- My child is fearfully and wonderfully made by God because his/her members are written in God's book.
- I prophesy that the child kicking in my womb shall grow up in the nurture and admission of God and shall serve God in the fullness of his/her destined capacity and capability in Jesus name.
- I bind every weapon fashioned against my pregnancy and declare that it shall not prosper in Jesus name.
- I nullify, make of no effect, scatter, uproot, destroy and throw down every satanic assignment against my pregnancy and the child in my womb in Jesus name.
- I shall not be too weak in body and soul to pray. I come against every satanic seed, spiritual poison, infirmity projected against my pregnancy and the child in my womb in Jesus name.
- I cancel the effect of food eaten in the dream meant to cause abortion, congenital disease or hard labour in Jesus name.
- I bind pre-eclampsia and eclampsia (hypertension in pregnancy), abnormal foetal growth and foetal organ malformation in Jesus name.
- I reject and take authority and dominion over placenta previa (abnormally placed placenta), blood group and Rhesus factor incompatibility in Jesus name.

- I reject ectopic pregnancy in my fallopian tubes in Jesus name.
- I come against congenital rubella syndrome, cord prolapse (umbilical cord before baby in child birth), an-encephaly (no brain) and hydro-cephalous (enlarged foetal brain and head) in Jesus name.
- I bind every form of child birth complications in Jesus name.
- I blindfold every evil eye, paralyze every evil hand and nullify every evil word spoken against my pregnancy and child in my womb in Jesus name.
- The child in my womb shall not be estranged by satanic evil spirits in Jesus name.
- I reject every negative DNA programme replacement in my pregnancy and child by remote or telepathic control in Jesus name.
- Nothing shall cast away my pregnancy in Jesus name.
- I bind the spirits of barrenness and unfruitfulness in Jesus name.
- I commit every three months of my nine months pregnancy into the hands of God and declare that it shall not exceed God's appointed natural time of nine months in Jesus name.
- I shall not be far from help during my labour in Jesus name.
- I cancel and bind all evil, witchcraft and occult hands of nurses, doctors or any other medical personal that shall come near me in Jesus name.
- I cover my pregnancy and child birth with the blood of Jesus.
- I reject excessive blood loss during delivery in Jesus name.
- I thank God for blessing me with a male (female) child in Jesus name.
- I begin to declare the revelatory name of my child......................... before birth and proclaim that my child shall grow with mental alertness, vitality and spiritual sensitivity in Jesus name.
- I vow to dedicate my child to Almighty God Jehovah and His Son Jesus Christ in the church of God in Jesus name.
- The child in my womb shall not be a delinquent, stubborn or rebellious child in Jesus name.
- I declare that he shall grow up to become a person of significance, repute, timbre and calibre in Jesus name.
- I prophesy that he or she shall be a blessing to society in Jesus name.

Victory Over Sinful Habits

- Father God I confess my sins of ………………… to you and ask for forgiveness. I claim the blood over my sins, faults and errors in Jesus name.
- I repent of every sin of omission and commission and promise not to yield my members (spirit, soul and body) as instruments of disobedience in Jesus name.
- Father help me to overcome temptation and every plan of evil spirits to make me fall
- I cast down every sinful imagination and pull down every stronghold of Satan in my life in Jesus name.
- I bring every thought emanating from my flesh and every thought projected into my mind and spirit to the obedience of the word of God in Jesus name.
- Sin shall not have dominion over me because the law of the spirit of life in Christ Jesus has set me free from the law of sin and death.
- Sin shall not conquer or bring me down and I proclaim that I am more than conqueror over the sin, iniquity and transgression in Jesus name.
- I bind every sin that is warring against my spiritual life and bring them under the blood of Jesus.
- I declare that I am triumphant over sin, death, hell and the grave in Jesus name.
- I bind every enticement of sin, carnality and the flesh and refuse to submit my will to every strategy of enticement.
- I reject and come against lust of the flesh, lust of the eyes and the pride of life in Jesus name.
- Father open my eyes to understand the mystery and effect of sin and help me to apply my heart to wisdom, knowledge and discretion.
- I come against every satanic bait, trap and snare of sin assigned against my destiny and life on earth.
- I reject every lifestyle that does not glorify God in Jesus name.
- I refuse to faint in times of trials and temptations in Jesus name
- I reject the fainting spirit of Esau that made him sell his birth right.

- I bind the spirit Jezebel assigned against my life in Jesus name
- I shall not succumb to every persecution assigned to make me deny Jesus Christ.
- Every friend, relative, co-worker, acquaintance or neighbour assigned to lure or entice me into sin shall not prosper in Jesus name
- I am redeemed from of generational curse of sinful habits in Jesus name.
- I break every recurrent cycle of defeat and failure as a result of sinful habits in Jesus name.
- I declare that I am a man/woman of integrity, honour and nobility in Jesus name.
- I hold myself in high regard and refuse to wallow in the mud of sinful habits in Jesus name.
- I am free from sin because the Lord has set me free indeed.

Victory Over Property Repossession

- I stand on the word of God that says,' wherever the soles of my feet shall tread upon has been given to me,' in Jesus name.
- I reject the repossession of my flat, house, building or landed property in Jesus name.
- Scripture declares that, 'Houses I did not build shall be owned and inhabited by me,' in Jesus name.
- I bind every set up in the realm of spirit against me to cause repossession of my property in Jesus name.
- My property is a gift from God and shall not add any sorrow to my life in Jesus name.
- Let the Lord rebuke every devouring spirit assigned to take my property from me in Jesus name.
- Let the angels of God and the Holy Spirit defend and prevent the repossession of my property in Jesus name.
- I overthrow, pull down, cast down, bind and issue a fleeing command to every spiritual giant assigned to evict me and occupy what belongs to me in Jesus name.
- I bind every spirit of the Amalekites, Zamzummims, Rephaims, Moabites, Ammonites and Philistines assigned against my dwelling place in Jesus name.
- I bind Satan and his principalities assigned against my area of abode in Jesus name.
- I declare that I shall not lack shelter over my head in Jesus name.
- I shall not be relegated from Landlord to tenant and rent payer in Jesus name.
- I take my portion of landed property from my Father God to whom belongs the whole earth, its fullness and the people.
- My property shall not be affected by the global economic recession in Jesus name.
- I call forth financial streams into my life and finances from every currency into my bank accounts in Jesus name.
- I shall not lack finances to pay my mortgage in Jesus name.
- I declare that I shall pay off my mortgage before the agreed term in Jesus name.

- I declare that the tenant(s) in my Buy-to-Let property (ies) shall not lack finances to pay rent in Jesus name.
- I reject stubborn, rebellious, dubious, quarrelsome, destructive and defaulting tenants in Jesus name.
- I call forth good, rent paying tenants into my property (ies) in Jesus name.
- I sanctify and cover my property (ies) with the blood of Jesus and declare that the spirit of repossession must pass over in Jesus name.

Victory Over Nightmares
And Bad Dreams

- I sanctify my bed and bedroom with the blood of Jesus and the fire of the Holy Spirit.
- I overcome every evil spirit assigned against me by night or day with the blood of Jesus.
- I shall not be choked to death or overwhelmed by the spirit of death assigned against me in Jesus name.
- Because the Lord is my light, my salvation and He is the strength of my life, I shall not be afraid of what the enemy can do to me in Jesus name.
- When the wicked, my enemies and foes rise up to eat my flesh, they shall stumble and fall in Jesus name
- My heart shall not fear but be confident, although a host of evil spirits shall come against me or stir up war against me.
- In the time of trouble or satanic attack God shall hide me in His pavilion and the secret of His tabernacle.
- No satanic spirit or agent assigned to plow upon my back with the intention of making long furrows shall prevail against me.
- I command every satanic finger assigned to plow on my body to wither and freeze in Jesus name.
- I nullify the effect of every mark or incision on my body in Jesus name.
- I shall not fall into any pit dug for me by my enemies. Those who dig a pit for me in the spirit shall fall inside that same pit in Jesus name.
- Every stone rolled against me shall miss its target in Jesus name.
- Every wild spiritual satanic beast assigned against me is defeated in the name of Jesus and I return them back to the sender(s).
- Just as Apostle Paul wrestled with beasts and overcame, I overcome every beast assigned to wrestle with me in Jesus name.
- Every beast assigned to wrestle with me in the spirit is defeated and overcome by the power of the Holy Spirit, the Greater One that dwells in me and by the blood of Jesus Christ.
- I leap over every wall, valleys, precipice, waterfall, mountain range, obstacle, barrier, flame, river, sea and battalion of troops assigned against me in Jesus name.

- My life is hidden with Christ, in God and His Holy Spirit.
- Because I dwell in the secret place of the Most High God, I abide under the shadow of the Almighty.
- I say of the Lord that He is my refuge and my fortress and in Him will I trust
- Surely God shall deliver me from the snare of the fowler, and from the noisome pestilence.
- My Almighty God Jehovah covers me with His feathers, and under His wings I put my trust.
- His truth is my shield and my buckler.
- I am not afraid of the terror by night; nor the arrows released during the daytime.
- Every spirit of infirmity assigned against me by day or night shall not prosper.
- No weapon formed against me shall prosper.
- Every spirit of calamity, failure, destruction, mishap, accident, plane crash or defeat assigned against me is cancelled, condemned and returned back to sender(s)
- Thousands of satanic assignments against me shall fall before they get close to me in Jesus name.
- Because I have made God my refuge and habitation, no evil spirit, plague, calamity, accident or untimely death shall come near my dwelling place in Jesus name.
- I thank God for His angels assigned to watch over me, guide me, guard me and defend me against danger.
- I shall not dash my feet against any stone, stumbling block or obstacle in Jesus name.
- I trample upon every young lion, lion, dragon, adder, leviathan, antichrist, red dragon, crooked serpent, fiery serpent and leopard assigned against me and my family in Jesus name.
- When I call the name Jesus every evil spirit assigned against me shall scatter seven ways.
- I nullify every bad dream and declare divine reversal of every satanic intention in Jesus name.
- I overcome every, witch, wizard, occultist, diviner, sorcerer, enchanter and demon principality operating in my community and city with the blood of Jesus and the power of the Holy spirit in Jesus name.

- I declare that I am more than a conqueror through Jesus Christ who loves me with an everlasting love.
- Lord, help me interpret every nightmare or bad dream and order my steps so I will not fall into every trap or calamity assigned against me in Jesus name.
- I release peace, sound mind, unconditional love, divine health, progress, forward movement, increase, enlargement, focus, vision, marital bliss, success, business breakthrough, open doors divine connections and divine favour upon my life and family in Jesus name.
- I decree that neither angels nor principalities, nor powers, nor things to come, nor heights, nor depths, nor any other creature, shall be able to separate me from the love of God in Christ Jesus.

Victory Over Insomnia
or Sleepless Nights

- I reject and bind every spirit of insomnia assigned against my life in Jesus name.
- I pull down every stronghold, cast down every imagination and bring every thought assigned against my mind to the obedience of Jesus Christ.
- I refuse to take thought for my bills, financial issues, mortgage payments or what I shall eat, drink or wear in Jesus name.
- I refuse to take thought for my school fees, pocket money, success in exams or pier pressure in Jesus name
- I refuse to take thought for my rent or monthly income in Jesus name
- I refuse to take thought for every pressure at work or business in Jesus name.
- I refuse to take thought for my children's upkeep, training and care in Jesus name.
- I refuse to take thought of the global economic depression in Jesus name.
- I reject every thought of harassment or past abuse in Jesus name.
- I bind every spirit of fear concerning marital abuse and violence in my home in Jesus name.
- I bind the spirit of anxiety, worry fear and doubt in Jesus name.
- I cast my cares upon the Lord because He cares for me.
- I command every satanic paraphernalia used to bombard my mind with negativity to be destroyed and to burn with the fire of the Holy Spirit in Jesus name.
- I reject and bind the spirit of self-pity and low self-esteem in Jesus name.
- I come against the spirit of rejection intended to make me dejected and secluded.
- The joy of the Lord is always my strength in Jesus name.
- I choose to rejoice and give thanks in every circumstance of life in Jesus name.
- I shall not be anxious for nothing but in everything through prayer and supplication with thanksgiving, I shall make my requests to

be made known to God and the peace of God that passes all understanding shall keep my heart and mind in Christ Jesus.

- The Lord shall keep my heart in perfect peace because my mind is stayed on Him.
- I think on things that are that are true, honest, just, pure, lovely and of good report in Jesus name.
- I refuse to be moved by evil report and choose to believe the report of the Lord.
- I shall not be moved although the mountains be removed and be cast into the sea.
- I refuse to be moved by what my eyes can see but what the word says that I have not seen yet.
- I depend on the revelation of the Holy Spirit and His word concerning what God has prepared for those who love Him.
- I receive the supernatural peace of God through Jesus Christ who is the Prince of peace.
- I receive the peace of God as given by our Lord Jesus and not as the world gives.
- I shall always sleep like a baby every time I lay my head to sleep in Jesus name.
- I receive sound sleep from the Lord because I am His beloved in Jesus name.
- Let the Holy Spirit quicken every part of my body that is not functioning fine in Jesus name.
- Every hormone in my body assigned to enhance my sleep process shall function fine in Jesus name.
- I plead the blood of Jesus over my brain sleep control centre and over every part of my body and bed in Jesus name.
- I shall sleep soundly and receive fresh revelation and wake up with vitality and strength in Jesus name.
- I receive the rest of God in my spirit, soul and body in Jesus name.

Power Over Charms, Spells And Enchantments

- I nullify every charm, enchantment, sorcery and divination assigned against my life in Jesus name.
- Every plan to invoke evil spirits against my life through charms, enchantments, sorcery, divination, crystal ball gazing and witchcraft shall not prosper in Jesus name.
- I nullify and plead the blood of Jesus on every charm or spell placed on my path, seat, table, room, vehicle or clothes.
- Just as no divination against Israel nor enchantment against Jacob prospers, so shall it not prosper against my life, family, job, business and ministry in Jesus name.
- The Lord shall make every diviner, charmer and enchantment mad and confused.
- The Lord shall frustrate every token of liars against my life in Jesus.
- I shall not be overtaken by the lips of talkers in Jesus name.
- The Lord shall keep me safe in the secret of His presence from the pride of man and shall hide me secretly in His pavilion from the strife of tongues.
- No weapon fashioned against me shall prosper and every tongue that shall rise in judgment against me is automatically condemned in Jesus name.
- I am redeemed from every curse placed on my life in Jesus name.
- As the bird in wandering and swallow in flying, the curse causeless shall not come in Jesus name.
- Every wind, whirlwind, hurricane, tornado or storms invoked against me is nullified in Jesus name.
- I close every pit assigned to open up its mouth to swallow me up in Jesus name.
- In vain the net is spread against the prey. The snare is broken and my soul is escaped as a bird from the snare of the fowler.
- I leap over every pit or wall and run through every troop in Jesus name.
- I shall not die but live to complete God's destiny for me in Jesus name.
- God causes me to triumph always through our Lord Jesus Christ.
- Greater is He that is in me than he that is in the world and I am more than a conqueror in Jesus name.

Nullify Generational Curses

- I dissociate myself from every generational curse in my family line in Jesus name.
- I nullify every generational covenant made in my family line with the blood of Jesus.
- I place myself under the covenant of the blood of Jesus and therefore make of no effect every other covenant that has been operating in my family line in Jesus name.
- I break free from every generational covenant by the power of the blood of Jesus and the name of Jesus.
- I bind every generational curse of low self-esteem and poverty in Jesus name.
- I bind and reject every generational curse of barrenness in all ramifications in Jesus name.
- I refuse to be held bound by the generational curse of retrogression, lack of progress and failure in Jesus name.
- I nullify every generational curse of a life of singleness and lack of marriage in Jesus name.
- Every generational curse of divorce in marriage is cancelled through the blood of Jesus and the fire of the Holy Spirit in Jesus name.
- Jesus has redeemed me from the curse of the law because it is written, 'cursed is any man that hangs on a tree, that the blessings of Abraham might come upon me; that I might have the promise of the spirit through faith in Jesus Christ.'
- The sour grapes eaten by my parents, grandparents, great grandparents and beyond shall not set my teeth on edge in Jesus name.
- I sanctify my spirit, soul and body with the blood of Jesus against every generational original sin of Adam and Eve in Jesus name.
- I renounce every generational sin of idolatry in my family line and pray that God would not visit the iniquity of my parents upon their children unto the third and fourth generation in Jesus name.
- I come against and nullify every congenital and generational disease in my lineage in Jesus name.
- I sanctify my DNA with the blood of Jesus and command every negative programme in my DNA to be wiped out in Jesus name.

- I replace every generational curse assigned against my family with generational blessings in Jesus name.
- Generations to come in my family line shall be zealous servants, followers and worshippers of God in Jesus name.
- I perpetrate a generation of those who love, serve and fear God and therefore, receive the grace, mercy of God unto a thousand generations in Jesus name.
- In the name of Jesus Christ our Lord and Saviour, I raise foundations of many generations, repair every breach and restore paths to dwell in.
- Because I fear the Lord and delight in His commandments, my seed shall be great upon the earth and my generation shall be blessed in Jesus name.

Victory over Retrenchment
And Job Loss

- I rebuke every spirit of the devourer assigned against my Job.
- I shall only lose my job if God is preparing a better one for me in Jesus name.
- Because I am a tither, God will open windows for me in heaven and bless me with a better job in Jesus name.
- I reject the spirit of fear because my life, times and destiny is in the hands of God.
- I refuse to put my trust in man because my help comes from the Lord in Jesus name.
- I shall not fall victim of envy, jealousy, segregation, racism or hatred in Jesus name.
- I shall not be moved although the earth shakes and mountains be removed and be cast into the sea.
- I shall not be ashamed in the evil time and I shall be satisfied in days of depression in Jesus name.
- I am a joint heir with Jesus Christ
- I am blessed going out and coming in
- I am blessed in the city and in the field
- I am blessed in my storehouse and basket
- I am the head and not the tail
- I am blessed with every spiritual blessings in heavenly places in Christ.
- My God supplies all my need according to His riches in glory by Christ Jesus.
- I ride upon my high place in Jesus name.
- A glorious high throne is the place of my sanctuary from the beginning.
- No charm, enchantment, divination or sorcery can remove me from my seat before my time in Jesus name.
- The Lord has placed people on my pathway in life to elevate, bless and favour me in Jesus name.
- The Lord shall make all things work together for my good and promotion in Jesus name.
- I thank God for making me employable in Jesus name.
- I am trusting God for the day I shall also become an employer of labour in Jesus name.

Overturn Unprofitable Business
To Profitable

- I ask God for wisdom to organize and move my business forward in Jesus name.
- I prophesy a divine reversal of every economic and financial crunch in my business in Jesus name.
- I ask God for divine revelation concerning the progress of my business.
- I bind every unprofitable spirit in Jesus name.
- I come against every evil spirit assigned to ground my business to a halt in Jesus name.
- I pray for wisdom and boldness to deal with unprofitable staff in Jesus name.
- I nullify every charm, incantation, enchantment and curses spoken against my business in Jesus name.
- I ask God for forgiveness in the area of tithing and repent from today in Jesus name.
- I rebuke and let the Lord rebuke every devourer assigned against my business in Jesus name.
- I pray for revelation, unction and anointing to change unprofitable attitudes, actions and decisions in my business in Jesus name.
- I call forth customers from the four corners of the earth to my business in Jesus name.
- Because I am not walking in the counsel of the ungodly nor standing in the way of sinners and my delight is in God's law, my business shall bring forth fruit in due season and whatsoever I lay my hands to do shall prosper in Jesus name.
- I call forth a master breakthrough from God in my business.
- I call forth contracts and finances from every currency of the earth into my business bank account in Jesus name.
- Strangers and sons of aliens shall feed my business financially in Jesus name.
- For my shame I shall receive double in Jesus name.
- I prophesy that this is the set time to favour my business in Jesus name.
- I call forth supernatural advancement, divine enlargement and forward movement in business in Jesus name.

- My God shall supply all my need in business according to His riches in Glory by Christ Jesus.
- God shall make all grace abound towards me for all sufficiency to abound to every good work.
- I refuse to accept failure and declare that I am triumphant and victorious in business.
- The Lord Himself teaches me to make profit in Jesus name.
- God gives me power and anointing to get wealth in Jesus name in order to establish His covenant of prosperity through Abraham and Jesus Christ.
- I receive the grace of God to turnover and make profit in millions of currencies in Jesus name.
- I pledge to pay my tithes regularly and commit some of my profit to the propagation of the gospel and soul winning in Jesus name.

Reject Gun And Knife Crime Against Your Child/Children

- I declare that no weapon formed against me or my children shall prosper in Jesus name.
- I bend and brake every bow of steel, arrows, knives, pistols, automatic weapons and guns assigned against me or my child/children in Jesus name.
- I declare that no bullet or weapon shall penetrate my child's/children's body in Jesus name.
- I bind, nullify and scatter every plan of weapons against my life, family and children in Jesus name.
- I scatter every man, woman, boy, girl or gangs assigned against my life/child/ children in Jesus name.
- We declare that a thousand shall fall on our side and ten thousand on our right hand side and it shall not come near us.
- I bind every spirit of bullying and oppression assigned against me (my child or children) in Jesus name.
- I ask for wisdom from God to choose friends for my child (children) who are not clandestine and covert in Jesus name.
- Let my child's/children's steps be ordered by the Holy Spirit as he/she/they goes/go to and fro school or park or gym in Jesus name.
- I pray that God would give His angels charge over my child/children in Jesus name.
- Let every incursion of gun or knife crime against my children be foiled and detected by the public, the law and police in Jesus name.
- I declare that no plague or calamity shall come near my child/children or dwelling in Jesus name.
- The Lord is our Shepherd, we shall not want. He leads us beside the still waters. He leads us in the paths of righteousness for His name's sake. Though we walk through the valley of the shadow of death, we shall fear no evil. He prepares a table before us in the presence of our enemies. He anoints our heads with oil, our cup runs over. Surely goodness and mercy shall follow us all the days of our lives and we shall dwell in the house of the Lord forever. Amen!

- The Lord is our light and salvation, we shall not fear what the wicked, enemies or foes shall do unto us.
- They shall all stumble and fall as they rise up to attack our flesh in Jesus name.
- I cover my child/children with the blood of Jesus.
- I decree that my child/children shall not be involved with gangs or cult groups in Jesus name.
- I bind and cast down every imagination or thought of gang or cult enticement in Jesus name.
- Lord grant me wisdom to train my children in your fear and admonition.
- I shall not bury any of my children in Jesus name.
- Nothing shall cut short the life of my children in Jesus name.
- Long life is the portion of my children and we are more than conquerors in Jesus name.

Teenagers Victory Over Gun And Knife Crime

- I declare that no weapon formed against me shall prosper in Jesus name.
- I pray for wisdom to deal with violent teenagers, classmates, piers and friends.
- I pray for wisdom for good choice of friends.
- I refused to be lured into gangs, cults, fights, alcoholism, substance abuse and sex.
- I see myself as a child or teenager with great prospects in my future.
- I reject low self-esteem and the spirit of fear.
- I shall grow up in the nurture and admonition of the Lord.
- I pray for the will power to keep myself pure and holy before God like Daniel who refused to defile himself with the portion of the king's meat.
- I thank God for the supernatural assistance to overcome the sword of the enemy, avenger and executioner.
- I am more than a conqueror through Him that loves me.
- I bend and brake every bow of steel, arrows, guns, knives, cudgels, clubs, pistols, automatic weapons and hammers assigned against me in Jesus name.
- I declare that no weapon, bullet or knives shall penetrate my body in Jesus name.
- I scatter every gang, violent and evil men or women assigned against me in Jesus name.
- Let God arise and let my enemies be scattered.
- A thousand shall on my side and ten thousand on my right hand side and they shall not come near me.
- I bind every evil oppressive spirit of bullying, verbal and physical abuse in Jesus name.
- My steps are ordered by the Lord away from gun and knife crimes in Jesus name.
- I thank God for angelic protection as I leave home and return.
- I shall not be apprehended by violent persons, gangs or groups during leisure time in Jesus name.

- Let the angels of God, law enforcement agents and Police foil every plan or incursion of violent teenagers and persons against my life.
- The Lord is my light and salvation, whom shall I fear. The Lord is the strength of my life of whom shall I be afraid. When the wicked, my enemies and foes shall rise up to eat my flesh, they would stumble and fall.
- I dwell in the secret place of the Most High and abide under the shadow of the Almighty. I confess concerning the Lord that He is my refuge and fortress, in Him will I trust. I shall not be afraid of the snare of the fowler, nor the noisome pestilence. God gives Hid angels charge over me. They bear me in their hands, I shall not dash my feet against any stone. I trample upon the lion, adder, young lion, scorpion, serpents, leviathan, crooked serpent, fiery serpent and leopards. No plague or calamity shall come near my welling. God shall deliver me because He has set His love upon me. He shall deliver me in times of trouble and with long life shall He satisfy me. I shall not die but live to declare the works of God.

Victory Over Segregation
And Racism

- I plead the blood of Jesus over every thought of racism in my heart and ask for forgiveness in Jesus name.
- I am the righteousness of God in Christ, therefore, I reject every form of segregation, nepotism and racism against my life in Jesus name.
- Nobody can reject me because of my race, colour, tribe or pedigree because I am made in the image of God.
- I am a joint heir with Christ and I am accepted in the beloved.
- If God be for me, nobody or system can be against me in Jesus name.
- Because I am a child of God, I am no more an alien from the commonwealth of Israel and the earth; neither am I a stranger from the covenant of promise.
- The blood of Jesus Christ has broken every wall of partition and I am no more a stranger or foreigner but fellow citizen with the saints and of the household of God amongst all nations.
- Because I believe in the Lord, I shall not be ashamed because there is no difference between male and female, Jew and Greek, bond or free; for the same Lord is rich towards all.
- No one can put me down because God has made of one blood all nations of men on earth and has determined the times and boundaries of their habitation.
- I decree that no one shall judge me negatively because of my race, colour or creed in Jesus name.
- I bind the spirit of racial prejudice and declare that I shall be judged in my job or business according to merit and not according to my colour or race.
- I come against the spirit of hatred and strife fashioned against me because of my race, colour or creed in Jesus name.
- I scatter and make of no effect every manifestation of institutional racism in my work place or business in Jesus name.
- I shall not be despised because of my colour or race in Jesus name.
- I pull down every obstacle placed in my path and break through every racial barrier in Jesus name.

- I declare that I triumph always against every racial scheme to overthrow me or nullify my efforts in Jesus name.
- I am more than a conqueror through Him that loves me.
- I have been redeemed from every curse of racism because Jesus Christ has redeemed me from the curse of the law and made me a child of Abraham and heir of promise through faith in Jesus Christ.
- I pursue, overtake and without failing recover all that has been denied to me as a result of racial prejudice in Jesus name.
- Since I am created and predestined according to the foreknowledge of God, I am called, justified and glorified in every area of my life in Jesus name.
- Nobody or devil can stop my progress as a result of racism in Jesus name.
- There is therefore now no condemnation for me because I am a child of God who walks in the spirit and not in the flesh.
- Henceforth, no one will know me according to the flesh but see me as a child of the Most High God.
- I pray for wisdom to handle other people of colour without racial prejudice or retaliation in Jesus name.

Victory Over Prison
And Detention

- I reject every spirit of confinement and caging in Jesus name.
- I may be in detention or prison but my mind is not in prison in Jesus name.
- I pull down every stronghold, cast down every imagination and high things that exalt themselves above the knowledge of God in my mind.
- I am more than a conqueror and I see myself leaping in the spirit over every wall and run through every troop.
- I command every wall of Jericho that is stopping my physical and spiritual and psychological freedom to crumble in Jesus name.
- God has caused me to triumph in every situation I face in life and He causes all things to work together for my good because I love God and I am called according to His purpose.
- I shall not miss my God given destiny because of my prison or detention time in Jesus name.
- I ask God to raise and prompt prayer warriors to intercede for me all over the world in Jesus name.
- I may be physically confined but not spiritually confined; therefore I rule and reign in my soul and spirit over my territories of influence in Jesus name.
- I shall not wallow in prison or detention in Jesus name.
- I pray for the right attitude towards others in prison or detention in Jesus name.
- I pray for opportunities of ministry to others in need while I am in prison or detention.
- Like Joseph I refuse to be angry with those who have brought about my incarceration in Jesus name.
- I pray for divine intervention like that of Joseph, Paul and Silas in Jesus name.
- I pray that God will use me to interpret someone's dream in prison or detention in Jesus name.
- I am victorious over the spirit of depression and seclusion in Jesus name.

- Because I dwell in the secret place of the Most High God, I abide under the shadow of the Almighty and I will say of the Lord that He is my refuge and fortress.
- I shall have the best report and favour from Prison and detention staff in Jesus name.
- Let God send His angel to set me free from imprisonment and confinement in Jesus name.
- He whom the Lord has set free is free indeed in Jesus name.
- I look into the perfect law of liberty which is the word of God and I shall be blessed indeed.
- I stand fast in the liberty where Christ has set me free.
- I proclaim the jubilee of God in every area of my life in Jesus name and I return to every divine inheritance belonging to me in Jesus name.
- I am redeemed from the curse of the law and set free from every spirit of legalism in Jesus name.
- There is therefore now no condemnation for me because I walk in the liberty of Christ.
- I declare that my life is hidden with Christ in God.
- I shall not die in prison or detention but live to declare the works of God and complete His destiny for my life in Jesus name.

Successful Immigration Application

- I ask God for supernatural intervention in my immigration application in Jesus name.
- I shall not compromise my Christian standards in my application in Jesus name.
- My application for permanent stay/work permit/HSMP/visit etc, shall not be rejected or denied in Jesus name.
- I bind the demon principalities ruling over the country of my intended stay, abode or visit in Jesus name.
- I plead the blood of Jesus over the satanic principality at the spiritual and physical entry gates of the country of intended abode, stay or visit in Jesus name.
- I bind every Goliath assigned against my free movement across international borders in Jesus name.
- I pray that God would assign His strong angels that excel in strength to scatter and clear the way concerning my application in Jesus name.
- My file shall not be missing or forgotten in the shelf or rack in Jesus name.
- I ask for divine favour on my application in Jesus name.
- Since the earth belongs to the Lord and the fullness thereof and every good and perfect gift comes from above, I declare that my application shall be granted from above in Jesus name.
- As long as I am mindful of God's call and fulfilling my own part in the divine commission, I receive my visa or stay in my divine destination.
- Wherever the soles of my feet shall tread upon, I possess in Jesus name.
- I refuse to be a fugitive in my Father's land in Jesus name.
- I bind the spirit of fear and intimidation in Jesus name.
- I shall not be denied of anything concerning my destiny in Jesus name.
- I flow in the abundant grace of God during my time of waiting in Jesus name.
- I prophesy that my time of waiting shall not be long in Jesus name.

- Like Daniel, Joseph, Moses and the three Hebrew boys of the fiery furnace, I shall be supernaturally favoured and elevated in my country of intended abode or stay in Jesus name.
- I ask God to give me the heathen for my inheritance and the utmost parts of the earth for my possession in Jesus name.

Success In Business

- I worship and adore you because you are my Alpha, Omega, Jehovah Jireh and El Shaddai.
- You cover me with favour like a shield and make my lines fall on pleasant places
- You are the portion of my inheritance and my cup
- You lead me beside still waters and into my green pasture.
- I receive from you the power, unction and anointing to make profit and prosper
- I receive divine knowledge, wisdom and understanding to prosper and grow my business.
- I declare that every talent you have bestowed upon me shall be optimized for business advancement.
- I receive unction for new streams of income and business breakthroughs in Jesus name.
- I am a kingdom builder and promise to commit a portion of my wealth and tithes for the propagation of the gospel of our Lord and Saviour Jesus Christ.
- I am destined to prosper empowered to succeed and armed to resist and overcome every satanic incursion against my business (es).
- I am a joint heir with Jesus Christ and heir of God.
- I receive the grace to multiply finances and increase in wealth.
- I possess the promises of God in a land flowing with milk and honey.
- I am triumphant over every financial challenge both spiritually and materially and bind the spirit of mammon assigned against my prosperity and progress.
- I bind the spirit of financial hardship of the end times controlled by the black horseman and I bind burglary, theft, fire, accidents and losses in Jesus name.
- I thank God for spiritual and financial open heavens; and rain upon everything and every business I lay my hands upon.
- I receive the spirit of entrepreneurship that was upon Abraham, Isaac, Israel and Joseph in Jesus name.
- I receive the supernatural ability for finding and multiplication of wealth.

- I am profitable to my generation and I shall contribute positively to the advancement of humanity and reduction of global poverty in Jesus name.
- I am blessed going out and coming in. I am blessed in this city. I am blessed in the fruit of my body and increase of my produce in Jesus name.
- I destroy every generational curse and cycle of failure, poverty, defeat and calamity in Jesus name.
- I shall not live a life of perpetual borrowing but be a blessing and lend to friends, relatives, church folks, communities, tribes, people groups and nations in Jesus name.
- I perpetrate a generation of blessed children, blessed wife, blessed businesses and replace every generational curse with generational blessings in Jesus name.
- Wealth and riches dwell with me and dwell in my house, family, business and ministry in Jesus name.
- I thank God for releasing the treasures of darkness and hidden riches of secret places upon my life, family and businesses in Jesus name.
- The Lord loads me daily with benefits and supplies all my need according to His riches in glory by Christ Jesus.
- I drink from wellsprings I did not dig, eat from vineyards I did not plant and own properties I did not build in Jesus name.
- I claim spiritual, psychological, and physical, financial, material blessings and territories in Jesus name.
- I operate in godly wisdom and excellence.
- The rock is pouring out oil upon my path and I wash my steps in butter.
- I receive supernatural, unprecedented divine favour from God and everyone who comes in contact with me in Jesus name.
- The blessings of God upon my life would not add any sorrow to it but add wealth, joy, righteousness and peace in the Holy Ghost.
- I am an employment provider and distributor of heaven's abundance in Jesus name.
- God's face is shining upon me and His countenance is lifted on me.
- I receive new realms and new dimensions of enlargement and increase in Jesus name.

- I bind the spirit of procrastination, distraction, abortion, disorganization and unfinished projects in Jesus name.
- I receive the finishing anointing from God for supernaturally assisted completion of every project I embark upon in Jesus name.
- Jesus Christ, the author and Finisher of my faith shall help me in the accomplishment of every project I embark upon.
- I shall not begin a project without finishing, travel without returning, pursue without overtaking, or lay foundations without completion in Jesus name.
- I press toward the mark of the prize of the high calling of God in Christ.
- I call forth currencies from nations of the earth into my bank accounts and areas of influence to enhance the fulfilment of my God-given destiny in Jesus name.
- My business shall expand from my community, nation, other nations and continents in Jesus name.
- I receive the grace to sow financial seeds to my Pastor, local church, body of Christ and my community in Jesus name.
- I receive divine grace for global philanthropy.
- I call forth more streams of income in the following areas; shops, chain stores, services provider and factories in Jesus name.
- I overcome Satan and his agents with the blood of the Lamb and the words of my testimony.
- I cover my job and businesses, premises, machinery, tools, vehicles, finances, bank accounts, contracts, connections, staff and family with the precious blood of Jesus that is speaking better things for me.
- I declare, proclaim, decree and prophesy that my business (es) is turning over and making profits in millions and billions of national and international currencies in Jesus name.

Declarations Over Your Tithes, Seeds & Offerings

As I pay my tithes, give offerings and sow seeds I am trusting God by faith for:

- Opened windows of heaven.
- Divine revelations, unction and anointing for increasing wealth and health.
- Spiritual rain upon everything I do.
- Knowledge for witty and scientific inventions.
- Unique and globally impacting registration of trademarks and patents.
- Good and fulfilling jobs.
- Divine promotion.
- Raises and bonuses.
- Supernatural debt reviews and cancellation.
- Accruing benefits and divine health.
- Restoration of lost days, weeks, months and years. I bind every palmerworm, cankerworm, caterpillar and mammon in Jesus name.
- Estates and inheritances.
- Tax rebates and repayments.
- Gifts and unprecedented financial favours.
- Cheques and financial remunerations in the mail.
- Payment of bills.
- Royalties from products and books.
- Divine rebuking of every devouring spirit.
- Righteousness, peace and joy in the Holy Ghost in Jesus name.

Prayers Against Tongues Of Backbiters, Gossips And Evil Spirits.

- I condemn every tongue that rise up in judgment against me in Jesus name.
- I shall not be overtaken by the lips of talkers, backbiters, gossips and spoilers of destiny in Jesus name.
- I return to sender every sharp sword assigned from the tongues of my enemies. Let their negative words return back to their bosoms in Jesus name.
- No spirit of condemnation shall prosper against me because the law of the spirit of life in Christ Jesus has set me free from the law of sin and death.
- Let every tower, gathering, table and altar of Babel erected against me be brought down, scattered, confused and burnt with fire in Jesus name.
- Their tongues and words shall be scattered in seven ways in Jesus name.
- I bind every spirit of witchcraft, occultism, demons and satanic principalities invoked through incantations, divinations, curses and evil words in Jesus name.
- I counter every negative word spoken against me by the blood of the Lamb and the word of my testimony.
- Let God arise and let their unclean lips and tongues be purged with coals of fire in Jesus name
- Let those who have desired my fall and calamity live to confess and propagate my testimony in Jesus name.
- They shall live to see my testimony and forward movement in Jesus name.
- I am redeemed from the curse of the law, generational curses, and curses of associations in Jesus name.
- In vain the net of tongues is spread against the prey. The snare is broken and my soul has escaped like a bird from the snare of the fowler in Jesus name.
- In Jesus name, I exercise spiritual dominance in the airwaves against every fowl of the air assigned to inject negative words into my mind in order to militate against my progress.

- I bring every thought into captivity, cast down every imagination, pull down strongholds in my mind and bring every thought into the obedience of Christ and His word.
- I counter every negative word from satanic agents and evil spirits with divine coals of fire.
- I am free to prosper and live my life in the word of God.
- I will not hear the voice of a stranger but always hear the voice of God, Jesus Christ and the Holy Spirit for divine guidance and direction in Jesus name.
- I release the blessings of God upon my life and family in Jesus name.
- I am pressing forward in life in Jesus name.
- I receive double and multiple blessings for every negative word spoken against me in Jesus name.
- I am triumphant over death, hell and the grave in Jesus name.
- I am more than a conqueror and accepted in the beloved in Jesus name.
- I am the righteousness of God in Christ and destined to win in Jesus name.
- He who has predestined my life has called me, justified me and glorified me in Jesus name.

Prayers for Diligence and Consistency

- I resist every manifestation of inconsistency in my life in Jesus name.
- I bind every evil spirit assigned against my consistency at work, business, studies and ministry in Jesus name.
- I take authority and dominion over broken focus, lack of vision and purpose in everything I lay my hands to do.
- I reject the spirit of procrastination in Jesus name.
- I refuse to quit from any divine assignment, project or business in Jesus name.
- Jesus the Author and Finisher of my faith would help me to be diligent and consistent in every assignment and project I lay my hands to do.
- I bind every backsliding spirit assigned against my endeavours in Jesus name.
- I will not look back or develop cold feet once I lay my hands on any project, business or assignment in Jesus name.
- I shall stand before kings and great men because of diligence and consistency in my life.
- God shall reward my efforts as a result of diligence.
- I shall continue to seek God diligently in every area of my life in order to receive divine reward in Jesus name.

Victory Over The White Horseman

- I bind the spirit of the white horseman responsible for end time deception in Jesus name.
- I bind the spirit of false prophets and false christs assigned against me in Jesus name.
- I shall not give heed to seducing spirits and doctrines of the devil in Jesus name.
- I destroy the projection of lying spirits and false doctrines shot from bow of the white horseman against my life in Jesus name.
- I seek to divide the word of God correctly through diligent study of the word of God and the right application of the principles of bible interpretation.
- I shall not listen to the voice of strangers, divination, enchantments, prognosticators and occult projections in Jesus name.
- No voice can snatch me from the hands of my Master in Jesus name.
- I nullify every silent, salient and audible voice of Satan and his cohorts in Jesus name
- I open up my spirit, soul and body to the voice of the Holy Spirit in Jesus name.
- I open my ears to the voice of the Holy Spirit for guidance, direction and fulfilment of divine purpose in Jesus name.

Victory Over The Red Horseman

- I bind the spirit of the red horseman militating against my life, family, job and business in Jesus name.
- I overcome the red horseman with the blood of Jesus
- I bind every blood sucking devil assigned against my life and family in Jesus name
- I come against blood thirsty and blood spilling devils with the sword of the Lord in Jesus name.
- I command the fire of the Holy Spirit to destroy the great sword of war, strife, contention, murder and anarchy brandished by the red horseman in Jesus name.
- Let the sword of the Holy Spirit scatter the sword of the red horseman assigned against my life in Jesus name.
- Let God arise and let all my enemies be scattered
- I bind every contentious and cantankerous spirit fashioned against me in Jesus name
- No weapon fashioned against me shall prosper.
- I bend every bow of steel, run through every troop and leap over every wall assigned to hinder my progress in Jesus name.
- I bind the spirit of quarrel and misunderstanding intended to remove peace from my life and family in Jesus name
- I bind the evil spirits responsible for contention and quarrel in my work place in Jesus name.
- I bind every spirit of misunderstanding, quarrel and contention assigned against my family and relatives in Jesus name.
- I come against the evil spirits responsible for church fights and church splits in Jesus name.
- I declare to every satanic storm against my life 'peace be still, in Jesus name.
- Let the angels of the living God fight and scatter every satanic principalities and powers assigned to cause wars and unrest in my country in Jesus name.
- Let there be peace in every nation where Satan is causing bloodshed and war in Jesus name.
- Let peace be restored globally, nationally and in my city in Jesus name.

- I challenge every incursion of the red horseman with the angels of God that excel in strength.
- I prophesy that Jesus already defeated every principality and power making a show of them openly and triumphing over them in it.
- Let peace rule and reign in my family, work place, church and community in Jesus name.
- I receive the peace of God that passes all understanding in Jesus name.
- I receive peace from the Prince of peace, Jesus Christ my Lord and Saviour.
- The Lord keeps me in perfect peace because my mind is stayed on Him.

Victory Over The Black Horseman

- I bind the spirit of the black horseman assigned against my economic and financial emancipation in Jesus name.
- I resist the spirit of poverty and lack in Jesus name.
- I bind the spirit of mammon responsible for the financial systems of the world in Jesus name
- I come against the devourer as I pay my tithes.
- Let the Lord rebuke every devourer assigned against my heavenly open windows in Jesus name.
- I overcome the stubbornness and strength of the black horseman in Jesus name.
- I shall not be affected by the global economic depression in Jesus name.
- I come against every austerity measure instigated by the black horseman in Jesus name.
- I shall not live a life of perpetual borrowing in Jesus name.
- I declare that every debt I owe shall be paid off by God's special grace in Jesus name.
- I shall live in abundance in a time of depression and austerity in Jesus name.
- I call forth well-paying jobs, business contracts and financial favours in Jesus name.
- I overturn every austerity scale of the black horseman in Jesus name.
- My bread, water and material wealth shall not be diminished in Jesus name.
- My God shall supply all my need according to His riches in Glory by Christ Jesus
- The Lord gives me power and anointing to get wealth.
- The earth shall not be as iron and heaven brass to my financial efforts in Jesus name
- I ask God to enlarge my territory of financial and business influence beyond my city and nation in Jesus name.
- I am an employment provider and distributor of heaven's abundance.
- I shall pay my tithes regularly, give to my local church and charity.

- I shall be a blessing financially and materially to my Pastor in Jesus name.
- Let rain fall on my land and everything I lay my hands to do in Jesus name.

Victory Over The Pale Horseman

- I bind the evil spirit of the pale horseman in Jesus name.
- I bind the pale horseman responsible for untimely and eternal death in Jesus name.
- I take complete authority and dominion over every evil spirit assigned to lure, mesmerize, frustrate and drag people to hell fire in Jesus name.
- I refuse to enter every gate of hell that Satan and his cohorts shall open before me in Jesus name.
- I shall not die but live to declare the works of God and finish well in Jesus name.
- I bind the spirit of error and willful sin assigned against me in Jesus name.
- I shall not tarry or wallow in sin in Jesus name.
- I command every mouth of hell that has enlarged her mouth against me to be shut in Jesus name.
- I stand on the blood and victory of Jesus Christ over death, hell and grave.
- I shall not be stung by sin and death shall not have dominion over me in Jesus name.
- I bind the generational curse of hell fire assigned against my family in Jesus name.
- I nullify every power of the pale horseman assigned to kill with the sword, famine, hunger, and beasts in Jesus name.
- I am more than a conqueror through Him who loves me and gave Himself for me.
- I am a candidate of heaven, fellow citizen of the household of God and a royal priesthood.
- I am predestined, chosen, called and justified by God.
- I shall partake of heaven's abundance and dwell in my mansion that has been prepared for me in heaven.
- I overturn every plan of Satan and his cohorts to bring apostasy and false doctrines into the generations of my family line in Jesus name.
- I shall receive commendation from my Lord and Saviour, 'Well done, thou good and faithful servant. Enter into the joy of my Father.'

- I declare that I am the righteousness of God in Christ, redeemed by the blood, the apple of His eyes and God's prized possession.
- I press forward to the mark of the prize of the high calling of God in Christ.

Victory Over The Edomite Or Fainting Spirit.

- I resist the spirit of Edom assigned against my Christian commitment, relationship with God, education, projects, business(es) and endeavours in Jesus name.
- I reject every fainting spirit of Edom assigned against my prayer life and bible studies in Jesus name.
- I refuse to give up at any little trial or opposition in Jesus name.
- Once I have put my hands on the plow, I refuse to look or turn back in Jesus name.
- I bind the spirit of unfinished projects assigned against me in Jesus name.
- I bind every fowl of the air and demons assigned to hinder me from reaching the finishing line.
- I can do all things through Christ t6hat strengthens me.
- I am an overcomer and more than a conqueror in Jesus name.
- Jesus the author and finisher of my faith shall assist me supernaturally in the completion of my projects, business contracts, education, heavenly calling and destiny in Jesus name.
- I shall finish well in a grand style in Jesus name.
- I bind the harassment of Jezebel against my God-given destiny in Jesus name.
- I shall not sell or mortgage my virtue, destiny, holiness, Christian testimony, birthright and conscience to the devil in Jesus name.
- I shall not lose steam before I reach the finishing line in Jesus name.
- Let God remove miserable comforters and hypocritical mockers assigned to hinder my faith and walk with God in Jesus name.
- My diligence and consistency with God shall bring me before great men in Jesus name.
- I shall receive the reward of diligence and consistency in my walk with God in Jesus name.
- I bind the spirit of Edom and the spirit of the bondwoman assigned to make me compromise in my time of waiting.
- I refuse every terror of the Philistines, Goliath and the bondwoman in Jesus name.
- Every spirit of Hagar and Ishmael must go in Jesus name.

- I ask God for the tenacity of Jacob who held on and refused to let go until he was visited by God.
- I shall wait on the Lord until my change comes.
- I shall renew my strength and mount up with wings as eagles as I wait on the Lord.
- I shall walk and not faint and run without getting wary in Jesus name.
- Lord, give me more strength and anointing to wait on you in Jesus name. Amen!

Missionary Thrust And Global Evangelization

- I shall participate and contribute positively to the expansion of the kingdom of God and propagation of the gospel on earth in Jesus name.
- I embrace the divine commission with my spirit, soul and body in Jesus name.
- I shall depopulate the kingdom of Satan and populate the kingdom of God on earth in Jesus name.
- I declare that I am a soul winner and evangelism promoter in Jesus name.
- The knowledge of the glory of God shall cover the earth as the waters cover the earth in Jesus name.
- In my time dry bones shall live again in Jesus name.
- I am the light of the world and the salt of the earth in Jesus name.
- Lord help me to make a divine deposit in the life of anybody who comes my way or sits by me in Jesus name.
- I bind every spirit of fear, intimidation and lack assigned against the evangelistic mandate in Jesus name.
- Let the gospel penetrate the 10/40 window which has the greatest population of the unsaved peoples and nations of the earth
- I prophesy that, 'from the rising of the sun to the going down of the same, the name of the Lord shall be praised in all nations of the earth
- I pray for salvation and the spread of the gospel in Fiji, Samoa, Tonga, Papua New Guinea, Solomon Islands, New Zealand, Australia, Micronesia, Indonesia, Philippines, Malaysia, Vietnam, Cambodia, Thailand, Myanmar, Bangladesh, India, Sri Lanka, Pakistan, China, Japan, Taiwan, Mongolia, Afghanistan, Tajistan, Kyrgyzstan, Kazakhstan, Uzbekistan, Iran, Iraq, Azerbaijan, Georgia, Turkmenistan, Syria, Turkey, Ukraine, Russia, Belarus, Poland, Lebanon, Kuwait, Quatar, Bahrain, United Arab Emirates, Oman, Yemen, Saudi Arabia, Israel, Jerusalem, Greece, Cyprus, Albania, Bulgaria, Romania, Serbia, Bosnia, Hungary, Austria, Lithuania, Finland, Sweden, Norway, Estonia, Denmark, Netherland, Belgium, Italy, Germany, Switzerland, France, United Kingdom, Spain, Portugal, Iceland, Greenland,

Nigeria, Cameroun, Gabon, Togo, Benin, Ghana, Ivory Coast, Liberia, Sierra Leone, Guinea Conakry, Guinea Bissau, Senegal, Gambia, Morocco, Mauritania, Mali, Algeria, Burkina Faso, Niger, Tunisia, Libya, Chad, Egypt, North Sudan, South Sudan, Ethiopia, Somalia, Kenya, Sao Tome, Canary Islands, Malta, Equatorial Guinea, Central African Republic, Democratic Republic of Congo, Congo Brazzaville, Tanzania, Malawi, Zambia, Angola, Mozambique, Rwanda, Zimbabwe, Namibia, Botswana, Lesotho, Swaziland, South Africa, Madagascar, Comoros, Mauritius, Seychelles, Reunion, Cape Verde, Canada, United States of America, Mexico, Belize, Nicaragua, Honduras, Costa Rica, Panama, Bahamas, Cuba, Jamaica, Haiti, Dominican republic, Antigua, Dominica, Santa Lucia, Barbados, Grenada, Trinidad and Tobago, St, Vincent, Guadeloupe, St. Kitis and Nevis, Columbia, Venezuela, Guyana, Suriname, Ecuador, Peru, Bolivia, Chile, Brazil, Argentina, Paraguay, Uruguay, Falklands, Islands of the seas, Arctic and Antarctica.

Apply the Precious Blood of Jesus Christ

- I plead the blood of Jesus Christ over my life, family, business, job, home, office, shop, vehicles, belongings and travels.
- When Satan, the death angel and evil spirits see the blood over my doors, windows, vehicle and home, they shall pass over in Jesus name.
- I apply the blood of Jesus over my spirit, soul and body.
- I apply the blood of Jesus Christ over everything I touch.
- I declare that because I am redeemed by the blood of Jesus, I pursue, overtake and recover lost years, lost materials, lost relationships, lost finances and lost destinies in Jesus name.
- I apply the blood of Jesus Christ over my going out and my coming in.
- I apply the blood of Jesus over my ears, feet, toes, eyes, mind, brain, and hands in Jesus name.
- Let the blood of Jesus speak better things for me in every area of life.
- Let the blood of Jesus speak life for me instead of death.
- Let the blood of Jesus speak progress for me instead of retrogression.
- Let the blood of Jesus speak prosperity instead of poverty.
- Let the blood of Jesus speak long life for me instead of untimely death.
- Let the blood of Jesus speak anointing upon my life instead of Luke warmness.
- Let the blood of Jesus open the Red Sea for me in Jesus name.
- Let the blood of Jesus fight for me in the regions of darkness in Jesus name.
- Let the blood of Jesus show up wherever my name is called for evil, harm, sickness, death and calamity in Jesus name.
- Let the blood of Jesus show up wherever my name is called for evil and blindfold every eye of Satan, satanic agents, principalities, powers, rulers of darkness, spiritual wickedness, princes of darkness, prognosticators, diviners, enchanters, crystal ball gazers, witches and the occult in Jesus name.
- Let the blood of Jesus make a way for me where there is no way.

- I command breakthrough by the blood against every satanic opposition against my progress in Jesus name.
- I apply the blood of Jesus Christ over every spiritual, psychological and physical graves dug by my enemies in Jesus name.
- I apply the blood of Jesus Christ over my sins, faults, mistakes, errors and shortcomings in Jesus name.
- There is no condemnation for me because the blood is speaking grace, mercy, forgiveness, life and prosperity for me in Jesus name.
- I apply the blood of Jesus Christ over every trap, snare, gin, pot holes and obstacles set against me in Jesus name.
- I overcome Satan by the blood of the Lamb and the word of my testimony.
- I cover my spouse, children, siblings, relatives and friends with the blood of Jesus.
- Let the blood of Jesus vindicate me before my enemies.
- Let the blood of Jesus show up in every secret and open enemy embattlement planned against me in Jesus name.
- I declare that the blood of Jesus is my answer and solution in every problematic situation in Jesus name.
- I declare and decree that the blood of Jesus is bringing abundant life to me in Jesus name.
- Lord, I thank you for the propitiation, substitution, redemption and reconciliation of the blood of Jesus Christ for my life in Jesus name.
- I shall not trample upon the blood of Jesus and make it of no effect but the blood of Jesus Christ shall be very effective useful in every area of my need.
- I am victorious over every challenge in life because of the blood of Jesus Christ.
- I wash my spiritual womb with the blood of Jesus for fruitfulness and supernatural enlargement in Jesus name.
- I cover and wash my body organs especially my lungs, heart, kidneys, liver, reproductive organs, and blood with the blood of Jesus Christ.
- I thank you for the blood of sprinkling, purifying and sanctifying everything I do and everywhere I go in Jesus name.

End Of Year Prayers And Declarations

- I thank God for seeing me through this year despite the challenges and plans of Satan.
- I thank God for His grace, mercies, protection, sound mind, divine health and progress in Jesus name.
- I ask for divine fulfilment of every promise, purpose and plan of God for my life during the remaining days of this year.
- I pray for total restoration and divine completion as the year comes to an end.
- I commit and cover every moment, second, minute, hour, day and month of the New Year with the blood of Jesus.
- I bind and cast out every evil spirit released and projected against my city during the end of year celebrations and satanic rituals.
- I bind every satanic spirit responsible for seasonal Hazards in Jesus name.
- I take authority and bind evil spirits of untimely death, vehicular accident, plane crash, gas explosions, suicide, terrorism and infant mortality in Jesus name.
- I declare and decree that the end of year celebrations shall be hitch free, peaceful and joyful in Jesus name.
- I declare that the New Year shall be filled with divine favour, divine connections, divine acceleration and divine accomplishment in Jesus name
- The irrevocable covenant blessings of Abraham shall be my portion in the New Year in Jesus name.
- My mouth shall be filled with testimonies in the New Year in Jesus name.
- I call forth new streams of income into my life and family in Jesus name.
- I bind the spirit of uncompleted projects, abortion, miscarriage of destiny and futility in Jesus name.
- The New Year shall be a year of financial emancipation in my life in Jesus name.
- I shall not default in the payments of my tithes and financial obligations to my church, charities and the poor in Jesus name.
- I bind the spirit of infirmity assigned against my life and family in Jesus name. We shall not languish in the bed of affliction.

- I bind and resist every generational curse, congenital disease, and recurrent cycles of failure, defeat, untimely death and calamity in Jesus name.
- I resist and bind every familiar evil spirit assigned to monitor and hinder my movements and progress in Jesus name.
- I pray for revival in my prayer life, intimate walk with God, bible studies and holiness in Jesus name.
- I pray for wisdom and understanding of the times and seasons of the New Year in order to flow in the prophetic manifestations and predestinations of God in my life.
- I ask God for wisdom to manage time and resources already made available for me in the New Year in Jesus name.
- I pray for the move and manifestation of the seven Spirits of God in my life during the New Year in Jesus name. I receive the Spirit of Dominion, wisdom, knowledge, understanding, counsel, might and reverence.
- I pray for focus and visionary walk with God during the coming year and pray for divine revelations and definition of the plans, purposes, projects, travels to embark upon and accomplish in Jesus name.
- I commit every event in the New Year into the hands of God Almighty and bind every satanic year planner for my life and family in Jesus name. I thank God for accomplishment of my personal year planner for the New Year in Jesus name.
- I call forth positive change in my job and business. Let God release better jobs and businesses, new streams of income, inventive and innovative ideas, promotions, favour with God and favour with men, divine expansion, spiritual, psychological and physical territorial enlargement, supernatural debt cancellations and repayments, gifts and bonuses, tax rebates, steady flow of financial income and supernatural harvest in Jesus name.
- I declare and decree in Jesus name that my heaven is opened and shall not be closed during the New Year in Jesus name.
- Let God rebuke every devourer for my sake and open the windows of heaven in Jesus name.
- I prophesy God's unconditional love upon my marriage, marital bliss, peace, unity, mutual understanding, fruitfulness,

commitment, fidelity and faith in my marriage. I call forth weddings and blissful marriages in Jesus name.

- I ask for angelic protection for every child during the New Year against paedophiles, accident, murders, bullying and gang attacks in Jesus name. Our children shall be spirit filled learning to walk in the ways and fear of the Lord in Jesus name.

- I ask God for the special anointing to fulfil his destiny for my life in the New Year. I pray for faith, resilience, tenacity, spiritual and physical energy, diligence, commitment and loyalty in the name of Jesus.

- I bind every storm, Goliath and obstacles assigned to resist my divine progress in the New Year in Jesus name.

- I pray for enlargement, spirituality and fervency in worship for my local church in Jesus name. I thank God for missionary and evangelistic grace upon my life and ministry during the New Year in Jesus name.

- I thank God for a greater grace in my prayer life in the New Year in Jesus name.

- I declare that sin, compromise and double standard shall not be my portion in the New Year. I ask for more grace for holy living in Jesus name.

- There shall be no manifestation of fiery and overwhelming circumstances in our lives during the New Year in Jesus name.

- There shall be no manifestation of untimely death in my life, family and church members in the New Year in Jesus name. Let every impending captivity, sorrow, tears and calamity be turned around as the streams of the south into victory, joy and testimonies in Jesus name.

- In the mighty name of Jesus Christ I bind and resist every satanic principality and power, manifestations of leviathan the crooked serpent, scorpions, lions, young lions, adders, vipers, dragons, false prophets and every spiritual beast that shall rise up against my family and I.

- I cast down imaginations, pull down satanic strongholds and bring every thought during the New Year into captivity to the obedience of Christ.

- The Lord shall crown your year with success.

Prayers Against Litigations And Court Cases

- I bind every evil spirit assigned to tannish my name and reputation through false acquisition in Jesus name
- I take authority and dominion over every plan of Satan and his agents to deplete my finances through litigation and court cases in Jesus name
- I pray for divine wisdom and spiritual understanding concerning any court cases levelled against me in Jesus name
- I ask for divine wisdom, counsel, knowledge and expertise for every lawyer, judge or magistrate handling my court case
- I take complete authority and dominion over every charm, spell, enchantment, divination and sorcery assigned against me by my accusers, prosecuting lawyers, magistrates and judges in Jesus name
- I bind the spirit of the accuser, avenger and envy militating against me in Jesus name
- Let God arise and let my enemies be scattered
- I condemn every tongue that rise up in judgment against me
- I bind and paralyze every gossip, lies and curses spoken and framed against me concerning this court case in Jesus name
- No weapon fashion against me shall prosper in Jesus name
- I bind every spirit of hired assassins, spin doctors and false witnesses and paralyze their human agents and weapons in Jesus name
- The Lord shall raise up faithful and true witnesses to speak for me in Jesus name
- I overcome Satan by the blood of the Lamb and word of my testimony in Jesus name
- I thank a God for divine favour from the jury, court staff, lawyers, magistrates and judges in Jesus name
- I bind the works of hypocritical mockers and everyone planning to take advantage of litigation and court case
- I pray for divine vindication and angelic assistance during the court case in Jesus name
- I plead and apply the blood of Jesus Christ on the court case, court venue and everyone involved in Jesus name

- I shall not be subverted from my course nor be denied my rights during any court case in Jesus name
- I pursue the court case with a heart of forgiveness for my enemies and accusers in Jesus name
- The Lord shall give me a word during trial that my enemies and accusers cannot gain say
- The Lord shall grant me victory and triumph at the end of it all

Prayers Against Long Standing Joblessness

- I bind all the evil spirits responsible for joblessness in Jesus name
- I shall not be forsaken nor beg for bread, rent or mortgage in Jesus name
- I destroy every generational and personal curses of retrogression, poverty and hardship assigned and spoken against my life in Jesus name
- I bind and reject the manifestation of personal negative traits militating against my job procurement and employment in Jesus name
- I bind the spirit of racism, segregation and nepotism preventing me from employment in Jesus name
- I reject the effect of prejudice, past failures and bad references in Jesus name
- I bind every satanic wall of unemployment around my life in Jesus name
- I ask for supernatural wisdom, knowledge and understanding to answer my job interviewers and employers in Jesus name
- The. Lord shall give me a word in season to answer every question
- Like Daniel in the Bible received from God, I ask to receive the spirit of wisdom, understanding, knowledge, dissolving of doubts and answering hard questions in Jesus name
- I plead the blood of Jesus Christ over my life, my job interviews and interviewers in Jesus name
- I ask for divine favour, grace and mercy concerning my job procurement and employment in Jesus name
- Let the floodgate of job interviews and gainful employment be opened in Jesus name
- I thank God for supernatural breakthrough for a very good job in Jesus name
- Let there be manifestation of God's perfect job for me in Jesus name
- Let the angels of God run to and for the earth to fish out His perfect job for me.
- The Lord shall make my face to shine before my interviewers and employers in Jesus name
- I thank God for a befitting and well-paying job in Jesus name

- I promise to be a regular tithe payer and giver to my local church when I get a job in Jesus name
- I pray for wisdom to manage my finances, spending and savings when I start receiving salary

Prayers Against Terminal Diseases

- Scripture declares that death and life are in the power of my tongue, therefore, I terminate every terminal disease assigned against my body and my life in Jesus name
- I return to sender every spirit of infirmity projected and assigned against my life
- I bind every satanic assignment associated with terminal diseases in Jesus name
- I shall not die but live to declare the works of. God and finish my divine assignment
- The Spirit of life in Christ Jesus has set me free from the law of sin and death, therefore, sin and death shall not have dominion over me
- Untimely death is not my portion because scripture declares that God shall satisfy me with long life
- I am healed by the stripes of Jesus from the top of my head to the tips of my toes
- I rebuke the demon of death in Jesus name
- I rebuke EBOLA, HIV, HPV, Breast Cancer, Brain tumor, Pancreatic cancer, Liver cancer, Abdominal and duodenal cancer, Leukaemia and every form of cancer in Jesus name.
- Let the Spirit of Him that raised Jesus from the dead quicken my mortal body
- No plague and no calamity shall come near my dwelling and body in Jesus name
- I bind every pestilence that operates in darkness in Jesus name
- The Lord has given His angels charge over me and I shall not dash my feet against any stone
- The Lord prevents me from sudden death and He covers my head in the day of battle
- I prophesy the life of God upon my spirit, soul and body
- Let the four winds that bring life from the Spirit of God blow upon my spirit, soul and body
- I speak life and spiritual rejuvenation upon every damaged tissue or organ of my body in Jesus name
- I declare creative miracle upon every damaged organ, tissue or bones in Jesus name

- Death has been swallowed up in victory when Jesus died and resurrected from the dead therefore, I shall not die but live
- I nullify the sting of death and power of the grave with the blood of Jesus and Jesus name
- The covenant of life I have with God destroys every generation curse and covenant of death in Jesus name
- I am victorious over death, hell and the grave by the power of the cross and the blood of Jesus Christ

Prayers Against Troubled Marriage

- I prophesy peace upon every spiritual satanic storm assigned against my marriage in Jesus name
- I bind every assignment of witchcraft, enchantment, spells, sorcery, divination and the occult against my marriage in Jesus name.
- I pray for wisdom, understanding and self-control concerning my marital issues in Jesus name
- I take authority and dominion over the spirit of rejection, pride and self-pity in Jesus name
- I pray for mutual understanding, concern for one another and compassion in my marriage
- I bind every spirit of hatred, carnality and insecurity assigned against my relationship
- I bind every strange man or woman assigned against my marriage in Jesus name
- I cancel the effect of false counsellors from friends, in-laws and relatives in Jesus name
- I reject and condemn every tongue that rise up in judgment against my marriage in Jesus name
- I bind the spirit of divorce and court cases assigned against my marriage in Jesus name
- I take authority over satanic strongholds and imaginations assigned against our minds in Jesus name
- I bind the spirit of lust, carnality, lies and infidelity assigned against my marriage in Jesus name
- My marriage shall not be a part of the national divorce statistics in Jesus name
- I put divine pressure upon every external being or spirit fighting against my marriage in Jesus name
- I take authority and dominion over any generational curse of strife, contention, separation and divorce spoken against my family line in Jesus name
- No weapon formed against my marriage shall prosper
- I bind the spirit of aggression and violence in my marriage in Jesus name

- I cover my marriage, home and marital bed with the blood of Jesus Christ
- No satanic or human power shall be able to cause separation and divorce in my marriage in Jesus name
- My marriage shall be conducted in honour and fidelity in Jesus name
- I pray for the spirit of power, love and a sound mind
- I pray for an open mind to godly counsel and the word of God in Jesus name
- I am not moved by what I see in my marriage but what the word of God says
- I cancel negative words, corrupt communication, curses and abusive language spoken against each other in my marital relationship
- My home shall be peaceable, quiet and sure habitation
- My home shall be a place of fellowship, prayers, divine revelation and safety
- Our children shall find peace, love, godly instruction, divine example and unity in my marriage
- I speak increase, fruitfulness, spirituality, and vision, destiny fulfilment in my marriage
- I prophesy life, peace, unity, marital bliss, unconditional love, meekness and humility upon my marriage
- My marriage shall be as heaven on earth in Jesus name
- My marriage shall long our lifetime on earth and we shall see our children's children in Jesus name
- We shall leave an inheritance for every seed of our marriage in Jesus name

Victory Over Barrenness And All
Forms Of Unfruitfulness

- I reject the spirit of barrenness and unfruitfulness assigned against my life in Jesus name
- Scripture declares that none shall be barren in the house of God therefore, I reject barrenness and unfruitfulness in Jesus name
- I bind every recurrent cycle of spiritual and physical abortion assigned against my life
- I plead the blood of Jesus over my physical and spiritual womb in Jesus name
- I speak the life of God upon my spiritual and physical wombs in Jesus name
- I destroy every chain, padlocks, strings and fetters assigned to tie my womb in the spirit world in Jesus name
- I command the fire of the Holy Spirit to burn every satanic and human assignment against my fruitfulness and reproduction in Jesus name
- I wash my physical and spiritual wombs with the blood of Jesus Christ
- I am a joyful mother/father of many children in Jesus name
- I shall give birth to God's plan and purpose for my life in Jesus name
- I command my fruitfulness to break forth like the morning sun in Jesus name
- Whatsoever I lay my hands to do shall prosper and bring forth fruit in its season
- My seed shall be as the sand of the seashore and stars of the sky
- All people and nations shall call me blessed and fruitful in every area of my life
- I shall not die with barrenness but produce fruit that glorifies God in Jesus name
- I shall dedicate my children and fruit to God with praise, worship and dance in the house of God.
- My seed and fruit shall be taught of The Lord and great shall be their peace in Jesus name
- I am fruitful in my body, soul, spirit, business, job and ministry in Jesus name
- I am redeemed from the curse of the law and partake of the blessings of Abraham through faith in Jesus Christ

Prayers Against Epidemics And Pandemics

- I prophesy against every spirit of infirmity responsible for epidemics and pandemics in Jesus name
- No plague and calamity shall come near my body, dwelling, community or nation in Jesus name
- I am not afraid for the pestilence that walks and darkness nor destruction that wastes at noonday
- Let the angels of God Almighty be assigned to stop every plague causing epidemics and pandemics in Jesus name
- I bind every satanic power responsible for societal, city, national and regional epidemic/ pandemics in Jesus name
- I plead the blood of Jesus over every epidemic and pandemic
- Let God arise and let the plagues assigned against His people be scattered and destroyed in Jesus name
- Let every plague causing epidemics and pandemics be destroyed from the roots in Jesus name
- No plague of bacteria or virus shall come near my body in Jesus name
- If any plague touches my body it shall dry up and die instantaneously because the spirit of Him that raised Jesus Christ from the dead shall quicken my mortal body
- I bind and resist EBOLA virus, HIV, HPV, Swine flu, mad cow disease, bird flu and every other epidemic and pandemic causing diseases in Jesus name
- I speak life to anybody affected by any epidemic and pandemic causing diseases
- I prophesy that they shall not die but live to declare the works of God and long life is our portion
- I pray for divine assistance in the discovery and production of vaccines, antibiotics and antiviral drugs that shall combat every epidemic and pandemic pestilence in Jesus name
- I bind every experimental accident or incident responsible for the spread of epidemics and pandemics in Jesus name
- I intercede as a priest between the altar and the porch against every plague, pestilence and disease causing epidemics and pandemics
- Let every plague and pestilence stop in Jesus name

Prayers for Consistent Christian Commitment and Service

- I pray for increased commitment and dedication to God in my Christian service
- I bind every spirit of Luke warmness, lethargy, distractions, nonchalance and worldly cares in Jesus name
- I shall neither be cold nor hot but be zealously affected in the good work of The Lord
- Let the zeal of the Lord's house consume my heart in Jesus name
- I bind every assignment of satanic evil spirits, witchcraft and the occult assigned against my destiny and Christian commitment in Jesus name
- I come against body weakness, sickness and depression assigned against my Christian commitment and service in Jesus name
- I bind every spirit of carnal pollution assigned against my commitment to God in Jesus name
- I bind the spirit of excuses and procrastination preventing me from fulfilling my divine assignment
- I shall increase my daily hourly commitment to serving God and doing the things of God in my local church.
- I shall pursue God's call for my life with zeal and dedication
- I press forward in my commitment towards the mark of the prize of the high calling of God in Christ Jesus
- I return to my first love with all of my heart
- I repent of every pollution of my heart by the spirit of Jezebel and Nicolaitans in Jesus name
- I shall not backslide because of hardship and satanic attacks
- I shall never deny Christ in times of persecution in Jesus name
- I shall finish well and receive commendation from the Lord, 'well done thou faithful servant'
- I am loyal, submissive and totally committed to my leaders and Pastor in Jesus name
- I hind the spirit of stubbornness, rebellion and selfishness in Jesus name
- I am a part of God's end time army
- I shall take the gospel to my community, city, nation and other parts of the world in Jesus name
- I shall be faithful to the end and finish well with diligence, excellence, prudence, efficiency and effectiveness in Jesus name

Prayers Against Sexual Perversion

- I reject and bind every spirit of lust, carnality and sexual perversion
- I sanctify my body, spirit and soul with the blood of Jesus Christ
- I declare that my body is the temple of the Holy Spirit and I refuse to defile the temple of the Holy Spirit in Jesus name
- I pray for the spirit of knowledge, understanding, wisdom and the fear of God upon my life
- I possess my body as holy unto God
- I reject and bind the spirits behind masturbation and pornography in Jesus name
- I come against every sexual act that does not glory God
- I bind every thought of paedophilia and sodomy in Jesus name
- I refuse to watch pornography channels on Television, social media and internet in Jesus name
- I cover my sexual and reproductive organs with the blood of Jesus Christ
- I am more than conqueror through Christ that strengthens me
- I promise to sanctify my body, spirit and soul for the Master's u

Prayers Against Sexual Harassment

- I refuse to succumb to every attempt of sexual overture against me
- I cover my body, spirit and soul with the blood of Jesus Christ
- I bind every evil spirit responsible for sexual Harassment in Jesus name
- I cast down every stronghold and imaginations of sexual lust
- I pray for repentance and the fear of God in the life of those harassing me sexually
- I pray that the person harassing me sexually would not see me as a sex tool but as someone with destiny and purpose in life
- Let the Holy Spirit touch those harassing me and make them detest me instead of lusting after me
- I possess my vessel in holiness and refuse to bow to every spirit of sexual harassment
- I pray for wisdom to handle sexual harassment and divine protection in time of harassment
- I bind that type of spirit that operated in the life of Amnon son of David who sexually harassed his sister Tamar
- I block every avenue in the spirit and physical world opening the door to sexual harassment
- I ask for wisdom to dress appropriately in a way and manner that would not be enticing to those harassing me sexually
- I bind every evil spirit of sexual harassment that would end up in rape in Jesus name
- I prophesy the mind of Christ upon my life that would prevent any sexual advances
- I prophesy that my body is the temple of the Holy Spirit and shall not be defiled but be sanctified for the Master's use
- No weapon of my attackers fashioned against me shall prosper in Jesus name
- I command every bow of steel assigned against me to the bent, arrows to be broken, knives to be blunt and guns to be locked in Jesus name
- I am not afraid of the terror by night nor the arrow that flies by day because the. Lord has given His angels charge over me
- I am more than a conqueror because greater is He that is in me than he that is in the world

- I have the spirit of power, love and a sound mind dwelling in me
- Let the Spirit of God visit and harass anyone trying to harass me sexually like the case of King Abimelech who was warned not to touch Sarah the wife of Abraham
- I thank God for deliverance from sexual harassment in Jesus name

Victory Over Enemies Of Progress

- I am pressing forward to the mark of the prize of the high calling of God for my life
- No satanic agent or power can stop me from going forward in life
- I bind the works of every enemy of my progress
- I take complete authority and dominion over every evil spirit of retrogression
- Where they have planned to cast me down or drag me backward, there shall be a lifting up
- Rejoice not over me O my enemy for I shall arise, shine and go forward
- The Spirit of Him that raised Jesus Christ from the dead that quicken my body against every debilitating and crippling evil spirit in Jesus name
- No enchantment and divination shall prosper against me
- The snare of my enemies is broken and my spirit, soul and body has escaped from the snare of the fowler
- I pursue, overtake and recover all that my enemies have stolen from my life in Jesus name
- I overcome every mountain, wall of Jericho, Red Sea, valley, crooked ways and rough places assigned to stop my progress to disappear and give way in Jesus name
- I bind and spoil every generational curse of retrogression, failure, defeat and near completion in Jesus name
- I bind, cast down and bruise the head of every spiritual Goliath assigned to intimidate and fight my progress in life
- I bind every satanic human agent assigned against my physical life and declare that no weapon of assassins, hoodlums, thugs, vehicles, and airplane shall prosper against my life
- I come against harassment by work colleagues, friends, neighbours, relatives, business partners and strangers in Jesus name
- I plead the blood of Jesus Christ over my glorious high throne, divine destiny and purpose in Jesus name
- The Lord shall prepare a table before me in the presence my enemies

- I pray that the spiritual eyes of my human enemies be opened for repentance and pursuit of God's purpose for their lives in Jesus name
- I bind every satanic spirit influencing my human enemies against me in Jesus name
- I shall not fall, I shall not fail, I shall not recede and I shall not die but live to see the glory of. God upon my life in Jesus name
- I shall live to be a blessing to my generation in Jesus name
- I prophesy promotion, increase, enlargement and forward movement upon my life in Jesus name
- I am supernaturally blessed, divinely elevated and favoured in Jesus name

Prayers Against Fraud And Fraudulent Persons

- I rebuke every devourer acting as fraudulent persons in Jesus name
- I cover my streams of income with the blood of. Jesus Christ
- Because I am in covenant with God, no fraud or fraudulent persons shall come near my business, job or finances in Jesus name
- Because I am a tithe paying believer, the Lord rebukes every fraud star assigned against me in Jesus name
- I shall not work and another eat my revenue, income or profit in Jesus name
- I bind litigation and court cases involving fraudulent persons in Jesus name
- I shall not be implicated, complicated or robed in by fraud stars during any work or business transactions in Jesus name
- The Lord shall prevent me from falling into pits and potholes dug by fraudulent persons against me in Jesus name
- I bind the spirit of greed, fast lane and get-rich-quick in Jesus name
- I pray for the spirit of knowledge, wisdom, understanding, discretion and judgment concerning every financial engagement or business proposal in Jesus name
- I thank God for discerning of spirits, word of knowledge and word of wisdom against every fraudulent relationship, union, business partner or sudden acquaintances in Jesus name
- I bind every carnal enticement assigned to lure me into fraudulent relationships on social media and internet in Jesus name
- My finances, job, businesses are blessed and dedicated to God Almighty in Jesus name
- Instead of fraud stars I attract those who shall enhance my work, business and finances in Jesus name
- I am blessed going out and coming in
- I am more than a conqueror in Jesus name

Prayers Against Blackmail And Sabotage

- I bind every satanic spirit of the accuser of the brethren in Jesus name
- I take authority and dominion over the evil spirit of envy, pride, bitterness and vengeance that triggers blackmail and sabotage in Jesus name
- I bind the spirit of the avenger in Jesus name
- I come against every gathering of saboteurs and blackmailers assigned against my life and progress in Jesus name
- I condemn every tongue of saboteurs and blackmailers and paralyze their weapons in Jesus name
- A thousand saboteurs shall fall on my side and ten thousand shall on my right hand side in Jesus name
- Let the angels of The Lord persecute my saboteurs and blackmailers in Jesus name
- No enchantment nor divination of blackmailers and saboteurs shall prosper
- Let God arise and let my enemies be scattered
- I bind every implication, complication and entanglements of blackmailers and saboteurs in Jesus name
- The snare is broken and my soul has escaped from every snare of blackmailers and saboteurs
- I return to sender every plan of saboteurs and blackmailers assigned against me in Jesus name
- Let their ways be dark and slippery and let the angels of God persecute them
- The Lord shall not approve of the plans of satanic spirits and human agents to subvert me in my course
- I declare that no power or influence can remove me from God's plan and purpose in Jesus name
- I shall not fail and I shall not fall because I am covenanted with God Almighty in Jesus name

Prayers For Divine Elevation And Greater Heights At Work And Business

- I thank God for divine elevation and greater heights in my job and business
- I resist every evil spirit of retrogression and stagnancy in Jesus name
- I bind every evil spirit assigned to put me under in Jesus name
- The Lord is my glory and the lifter up of my head
- I arise and shine because my time and my light has come in Jesus name
- The Lord shall bless the works of my hands a thousand times and I shall go forward, grow and become very great in Jesus name
- I call forth promotion from The Lord in everything I lay my hands to do
- The set time to favour me has come in Jesus name
- I am blessed and highly favoured for promotion, increase and enlargement in Jesus name
- Every see I have sown shall lead to exponential growth and increase in Jesus name
- I am sitting together with Jesus Christ in heavenly places therefore, no satanic power or agent can bring me down
- I am victorious and triumphant over failure, demotion, error and untimely death in Jesus name
- I ride upon my high places in spiritual, heavenly and earthly places in Jesus name
- I am the head and not the tail
- I am above only and not beneath
- I leap over every wall and run through every troop in Jesus name
- I thank God for fulfilling His plans and purpose for my life

Prayers For Divine Favour With National Rulers, Presidents, Governors And Corporate Leaders

- I declare that a people and rulers I do not know shall favour me in Jesus name
- My lines shall fall on high and pleasant places
- I bind every satanic obstacle assigned to block my favour and emancipation in Jesus name
- I pray for supernatural opening of doors of favour
- I break through every relationship barrier preventing me from meeting rulers and corporate leaders assigned to be part of my destiny
- I shall appear before leaders in high places like Joseph appeared before Pharaoh and Daniel appeared before Nebuchadnezzar
- Queens of Sheba and Seba shall enhance my destiny in Jesus name
- Let the favour on Esther for unmerited favour come upon my life in Jesus name
- My days and years of labour shall be overtaken by sudden favour in Jesus name
- God has covered me with favour like a shield
- I am blessed, divinely and highly favoured
- I shall be favoured by Men of God, Kings, Queens, Princes, Princesses, Presidents, Prime Ministers, Governors, Mayors, Parliamentarians, Senators, Judges, Stars, CEOs, Chairmen and Professionals
- I declare that my set time of favour has come

Prayers For Debt Repayment And Cancellation

- I pray for wisdom and and self-discipline for debt repayment
- I ask God for consistency in repayments of my debts
- I am believing God for debt cancellation and rescheduling in Jesus name
- I pray for extra streams of income to enable me pay off my debts in record time
- I bind every devouring spirit that would cause my debts to increase
- I receive knowledge for witty inventions that would bless others and increase my income
- I pray for wisdom and tenacity in saving a tenth of my income and paying off my debts with 30% of my income monthly
- I shall not default in the payment of my tithes and giving to charity and my local church
- I bind every spirit of palmerworms, locusts, caterpillars and cankerworms assigned against my finances in Jesus name
- I shall not live a perpetual life of borrowing
- I shall not default in the repayment of my mortgages but repay before full term
- I bind every devouring activity that would incur debts through accidents, burglary, fire, theft, illness and fraud
- My job and businesses shall be stable and profitable in Jesus name
- I shall leave an inheritance for my children's children in Jesus name
- I am blessed, divinely favoured and supernaturally elevated in Jesus name
- I thank God for divine jubilee over my finances

Prayers for Holidays and School Trips

- I pray for divine protection throughout my holidays and children's school trips
- I cover my family holiday trip with the blood of Jesus Christ
- I bind the activities of blood spilling evil spirits manifested as accidents and plane crash in Jesus name
- I commit the heart of every driver of my vehicles and pilots of my airplane into the hands of God
- I bind the spirit of error and calamity during my holidays
- I pray that my children's school trip shall be fill with knowledge, enlightenment and refreshment
- I reject every assignment of evil men and women against my holiday and children's school trip in Jesus name
- No plague and no calamity shall come near my dwelling place in Jesus name
- I shall not come back from holidays with depression, sickness or injury
- I bind the activities satanic principalities and powers against my family in my holiday destination and abode in Jesus name
- I take authority and dominion over minor bodily injuries, theft and burglary during my holidays and children's school trips in Jesus name
- I thank God for a safe trip and journey mercies
- I thank God for divine connections and favours during my holidays and children's school trips
- No weapon fashioned against me during my holidays and children's school trips shall prosper
- I thank God for financial prudence during my holidays
- My holidays and children's school trips shall be restful and fulfilling in Jesus name

Prayers Against Stubborn Tenants

- I pray for good, loyal and God-fearing tenants
- I bind the spirit of rebellion, disobedience and vandalism assigned against my tenant(s) in Jesus name
- I reject stubborn tenants in Jesus name
- I pray for a good relationship with my tenant(s)
- I declare that my tenant(s) shall fulfil their part of the tenancy agreement
- I cover my rented accommodation with the blood of Jesus Christ and declare that no illegal activity shall be perpetrated in it
- I bind the activities of evil spirits roaming in the region of my rented accommodation and declare that they shall not be able to perform their enterprise in Jesus name
- I replace every stony heart with a heart of flesh
- I bind every act of arson and vandalism in my rented accommodation
- I pray for divine touch on the life of my tenant(s) in Jesus name
- I declare that the tenure of my tenant(s) shall be mutually beneficial in Jesus name
- I reject occult, witchcraft, covert and clandestine activities in my rented accommodation in Jesus name
- I come against illegal activities in my rented accommodation in Jesus name
- I declare that my tenant(s) would not default in payment of rent
- I bind every subversive tenant activity in Jesus name
- I pray for mutual respect and humility in the life of my tenant(s)

Prayers Against Stubborn Landlords

- I pray for a God-fearing landlord in Jesus name
- I pray for a considerate and caring landlord in my rented accommodation
- My landlord shall not be a taskmaster or Shylock in Jesus name
- I pray that my landlord shall fulfil his on part of our tenancy agreement in Jesus name
- I pray for a good relationship with my landlord
- I bind every resistance and stubbornness in the life of my landlord in Jesus name
- I receive divine favour from my landlord in Jesus name
- Lord help me to act and conduct myself in a manner that is pleasing to my landlord

Prayers Against Long-standing And Recurrent Issues

- I consistently commit every long-standing and recurrent issues in my life into the hands of God
- I declare that nothing in my life shall be impossible with God
- I bind and scatter every satanic influence against my life in Jesus name
- I cast down every imagination and stronghold in my life in Jesus name
- I command every Red Sea and Wall of Jericho preventing my progress to give way and crumble in Jesus name
- I shall not be discouraged but renew my strength in my time of waiting
- I shall continue to stand firm and serve God with all my heart as I wait upon the Lord
- No issue in my life shall prevent me from fulfilling my divine destiny in Jesus name
- Let the anointing of the Holy Spirit destroy every yoke and burden of Satan assigned against my life
- Let every mountain in my life be levelled, valleys exalted, crooked ways made straight and rough places smooth in Jesus name
- I receive the easy yoke and light burden from the Lord in Jesus name
- I declare that I am free from every lawful captivity of Satan
- I command a release from every captivity of the terrible in Jesus name
- I am not a prey of the terrible in Jesus name
- I see and rejoice in advance for my day of testimony
- I invoke the powers of Jehovah and His Son Jesus Christ against every satanic resistance
- Let God opened the two leaved gates and break in pieces the gates of brass and bars of iron
- The Lord shall turn around every captivity in my life and put laughter in my mouth in Jesus name
- I declare that I shall reap in joy because I have sown in tears
- God makes all my life circumstances to work together for my good
- I shall end up with my harvest and breakthrough in Jesus name
- God's grace is sufficient for me in Jesus name

Prayers Of Destabilization Against Satanic Powers

- I put confusion in the camp of Satan and let them begin to fight themselves in Jesus name
- I send and throw the fire of God upon every satanic gathering assigned against my life, family, church, job and business
- Let every satanic altar holding my name be burnt to ashes in Jesus name
- I burn and scatter every spiritual chain, fetters and bands assigned against me in Jesus name
- Let God arise and let all my enemies be scattered
- Let God discomfit every satanic opposition against my life with lightning, thunder, fire and brimstone in Jesus name
- Let the angels of The Lord persecute every satanic host assigned against my progress in Jesus name
- Let their ways be dark and slippery in Jesus name
- Let the angels of Satan assigned against my life miss their target in Jesus name
- A thousand satanic host shall fall on my side and ten thousand shall fall on my right hand side in Jesus name
- I am triumphant and victorious over the powers of darkness assigned against my life
- God's grace is sufficient for me in Jesus name

Prayers Against The Spirit Of The Avenger

- I resist the spirit of the avenger against my life, freedom and emancipation in Jesus name
- I bind every spirit of envy that attracts the avenger against my life in Jesus name
- I declare that the spirit of the avenger shall not have any access into my life in Jesus name
- I block every assignment of the spirit of the avenger through my relatives, friends, acquaintances and church members
- I shall not take vengeance into my hands but allow the Holy Spirit and God's angels fight my battles
- I pray for anointing, knowledge, wisdom, understanding and discerning of spirits to deal with the spirit of the avenger in Jesus name
- I pray for divine vengeance and vindication in Jesus name
- Let God Almighty avenger my avengers in Jesus name
- I bind every communal, national and international cross fires of the avenging spirits assigned against my life in Jesus name
- I shall not be caught in the cross fire of the spirit of the avenger in Jesus name
- I condemn every tongue of gossip and liars rising in judgment against me in Jesus name
- Let God set me free from every entanglement of the spirit of the avenger in Jesus name
- Let the blood of Jesus Christ protect me from every secret and open attack of the spirit of the avenger against my life
- Let the angels of God surround and protect me from the vicious and evil spirit of the avenger
- I declare that no human agent of the spirit of the avenger shall prosper against me in Jesus name
- God shall open my spiritual eyes to detect every avenger in Jesus name
- Let every agent of the avenger pretending to be my friend and helper be exposed and disgraced in Jesus name
- No stray bullet or weapon shall prosper against me in Jesus name
- I shall not travel in any boat, vehicle or aircraft marked and targeted by the spirit of the avenger in Jesus name

- My identity shall not be mistaken by agents of the spirit of the avenger in Jesus name
- My good shall not be evil spoken and nobody shall reward my good with evil in Jesus name
- I pray for divine protection against terrorist, murderers, mobs and gangs in Jesus name
- My life shall not be cut short by the agents of the spirit of the avenger
- I bind the activities of the spirit of the avenger through my boss, leader, co-workers and passers-by in Jesus name
- Out of the mouth of babes, God shall ordain strength to still the mouth of the avenger in Jesus
- I prophesy doom and confusion against the avenger in Jesus name
- My avengers shall not be able to perform their enterprise in Jesus name
- I turn backward and nullify every counsel and intention of my avengers in Jesus name
- My avengers shall come against me one way but flee and scatter seven ways
- Let the angels of the Lord persecute my avengers and the spirits working with them in Jesus name
- No plan of my avengers shall see the light of day
- I am divinely protected from every arrow of my avengers because I dwell in the secret place of the most High God and abide under His shadow
- I say of the Lord that He is my refuge and fortress
- I am not afraid of the snare of the avenger because God covers me with His feathers
- I am not afraid for the terror by night nor arrow that flies by day
- I trample upon the avenging lion, young lion, serpent, scorpion and adder in Jesus name
- The Lord shall avenge me of all my enemies and avengers in Jesus name

Prayers Against Eating Disorders And Weight Problems

- I pray for divine knowledge, wisdom and understanding for healthy dieting
- My body shall maintain a healthy balanced diet utilizing every food item naturally provided to nourish my body
- I take authority in the name of Jesus Christ over every form of genetic and self-induced eating disorders including Bulimia, kwashiorkor, rickets, osteoporosis, obesity, gout, avitaminosis, glaucoma, atherosclerosis and cancer
- I bind the spirit of infirmity and cover my spirit, soul and body with blood of Jesus
- I shall not poison or destroy my body with excess carbohydrate, palatable junk food, sugar, unsaturated fat, bad cholesterol, etc.
- I pray for self-control in the consumption of carbohydrates, fats and sugar in order to reduce my body weight
- I pray for craving and desire for vegetables, salads, plant proteins and anti-oxidants
- I pray for healthy eating knowledge and habit that will help me leave a healthy life and maintain my body weight
- I shall not defile my body which is the temple of the Holy Spirit
- I bind every satanic plan and craving for dangerous foods that will cut my life short
- I take complete authority and dominion over substance abuse like smoking, alcoholism and drug addiction causing depression, sickness and untimely death
- I reject, cast out, and nullify every satanic dainty or meal offered to me in the spirit realm
- I refuse to eat from the table of idols
- If I eat any deadly, poisonous and infected food, it shall not harm me in Jesus name
- I pray to embark on spiritual and detoxifying fast that would boost my health
- Whatever enters my body is holy, pure and blessed in the name of Jesus Christ
- I shall not die but live to declare the works of God and long life is my portion
- I desire foods that make me physically, strong, mentally alert and spiritually sensitive

Prayers For Single Parents, Widows And Widowers

- I pray for divine support for my family and children in Jesus name
- My God shall supply all my family need according to His riches in glory by Christ Jesus
- As a widow, I declare that God is my husband, comforter provider, protector and helper of my family
- As a widower, I declare that God is my comforter, provider, protector and helper of my family
- As a single parent, I declare that God is my provider, protector and helper of my family
- My family shall not lack nor beg for bread
- I pray for grace and strength to sanctify my spirit, soul and body for the Master's use
- I shall not allow carnal and lustful cravings take control of my actions bind every satanic assignment against my life and family in Jesus name
- I refuse to defile my body while I wait on the Lord
- I declare and pray that God shall provide me with a life partner that loves and fears the Lord at the appropriate time in Jesus name
- I vow to serve and love the Lord all the days of my life
- My children and family shall be brought up with godly precepts and counsel in Jesus name
- The Lord is my Shepherd therefore, I shall not want
- God is my glory and the lifter up of my head

Prayers For Elderly Senior Citizens

- I thank God for the gift of long life
- I thank God for preserving, protecting and providing for me
- I thank God for care-ers and helpers in my old age
- Like Caleb, I shall serve The Lord in my old age with consistency and fervency
- I shall not be weak, frail or sickly in my old age
- I can do all things through Christ that strengthens me
- I pray for knowledge and wisdom for a healthy geriatric (old age) diet in Jesus name
- My bones shall not be porous, weak or brittle in Jesus name
- I speak strength to my joints and bones in Jesus name
- I prophesy fire in my bones
- I bind every geriatric disease in Jesus name
- I declare that no one shall take advantage of my old age to abuse or harm me in Jesus name
- The Lord shall give His angels to take care of me at all times in Jesus name
- The Lord shall make all things work together for my good and I am more than a conqueror
- I my old age, I shall eat the fruit of my labour
- My children, friends and acquaintances shall not abandon me during my old age
- I shall reap every good seed sown during my life
- I am blessed and shall be blessed in my old age because I have been a blessing to my children, friends and acquaintances
- I pray for proper knowledge and wisdom to maintain a healthy life style especially for my teeth, bones, joints, brain, kidneys and heart.
- I pray for unction and consistency in my daily physical exercises
- I shall be a blessing to my children and generation in my old age
- I shall be a source of godly instruction and counsel to generations behind me
- I shall leave a legacy of the gospel and godly example to generations behind me
- I thank God for secular and divine gratuity and pension that would provide my need in my old age

- Because I am a a righteous and good person, I shall leave an inheritance for my children and grandchildren in Jesus name
- The Lord shall not forsake me in my old age but anoint me to finish well
- I shall complete my divine destiny in Jesus name
- I pray to continue my life with God in heaven when He pleases to call me home in Jesus name

Prayers Against Stress

- I thank God for divine peace upon my life, business and job
- The Lord shall keep me in perfect peace because my mind is stayed on Him
- I reject every form of self-induced stress
- I bind every stress induced by evil spirits in Jesus name
- I refuse to allow anxiety, fear and doubt rule my life
- I take authority and dominion over every stress that would cause hypertension in my body in Jesus name
- Let the peace of God keep my heart and kind in Christ Jesus
- I cast my cares upon the Lord because He cares for me
- I speak peace upon every spiritual storm or hurricane assigned against my life in Jesus name
- I cast down every imagination, pull down every stronghold and bring every thought into captivity to the obedience of Christ
- I am blessed and stress free in Jesus name
- I thank God for faith and boldness against every spirit of fear, doubt, anxiety and worry in Jesus nam

Prayers Against Terrorism

- I thank God for divine protection wherever I go
- No weapon fashioned against me shall prosper
- I am not afraid of the terror by night nor arrow that flies by day
- A thousand terrorists shall fall by my side and ten thousand by my right hand side
- I am more than a conqueror and triumphant over every plans of terrorists against my life
- I bind the spirit of the avenger manifesting as terrorists assigned against my life
- I trample upon every serpent and scorpion assigned against me in Jesus name
- I am victorious and triumphant over death, grave and hell in Jesus name
- My presence and body dispels and repels every terrorist from my vicinity
- I take authority and dominion over suicide bombers in Jesus name
- I shall not enter any building, vehicle or aircraft targeted or inhabited by terrorists in Jesus name
- I bind the spirit of the bond woman assigned against me in Jesus name
- The Lord shall give His angels charge over me
- I possess, rule and reign wherever the souls of my feet shall thread upon
- Let every cudgel, knife, machete, gun and bomb assigned against me return to the bosom of the sender in Jesus name
- I bind every terrorism assigned against my community, city and nation in Jesus name
- I bind mass murder and death in my country as a result of terrorist activities in Jesus name
- I thank God for divine arrest and extermination of terrorist groups in Jesus name
- Because the Lord is my light and salvation, I shall not fear what my foes, enemies and wicked shall do unto me
- The Lord keeps me safe in his hands and I dwell in His secret place

Prayers for those Seeking Accommodation

- I pray for divine leading and direction to my suitable accommodation
- I pray for a good, reasonable and inexpensive accommodation
- My accommodation shall be a peaceable and quiet dwelling place
- I bind every evil spirit that has or is inhabiting the flat or house where I shall dwell
- I bind generation demons and evil covenants perpetrated in my place of future abode
- I apply the blood of Jesus upon my prospective accommodation
- I am trusting God for a good and understanding landlord
- I shall not dwell in any flat or house doomed for calamity in Jesus name
- I pray for divine favour and open heavens wherever I stay
- My lines shall fall on pleasant places because I have a good heritage
- I am trusting God to move from my prospective accommodation to my own flat or house in Jesus name
- So help me God!

OTHER BOOKS PUBLISHED BY
THE FOURTH MAN PUBLICATIONS

The Successful Christian Businessman & Woman

The Da Vinci Code Truly Fiction

Children Are Like Olive Plants

Overcoming in Gilgal

33 Tips for Single Ladies

A-Z of the Multipurpose Woman

Making Progress

Victory Over Offences

Designed for the Palace

Inspirational Business Ideas

For further information and other ministry products contact pastorclem@triumphant.org.uk or pastormarjorie@triumphant.org.uk